ב״ה

CHASSIDIC SOUL REMEDIES

INSPIRATIONAL INSIGHTS FOR LIFE'S DAILY CHALLENGES

By
Rabbi Dovid Shraga Polter

SICHOS IN ENGLISH
788 EASTERN PARKWAY
BROOKLYN, NEW YORK 11213

ה׳תשס״ד • 2004

CHASSIDIC REMEDIES

Published and Copyrighted © by
SICHOS IN ENGLISH
788 EASTERN PARKWAY • BROOKLYN, N.Y. 11213
TEL. (718) 778-5436
EMAIL: SIE100@AOL.COM

RABBI DOVID SHRAGA POLTER
24641 CHURCH • OAK PARK, MI 48237
TEL. (248) 967-6910
EMAIL: DSP107@SBCGLOBAL.NET

ISBN 1-8814-0076-X

5764 • 2004

TABLE OF CONTENTS

AUTHOR'S
FOREWORD

This book was born out of my own search for strength and inspiration. In times of spiritual need, I have turned to our chassidic writings for direction and guidance. Seeing the results in my life and in the lives of others with whom I have shared these treasures, I came to the realization that a collection of selected stories and teachings would be uplifting and encouraging to my fellow Jews.

Someone may ask, "How do these stories relate to me? After all, they are dealing with holy people who stood on a much higher level than the average person."

Regarding chassidic stories, the Rebbe has said: "If, by Divine Providence, these stories have been passed down to us, this is a clear indication that they apply to us, too. Being a Jew with a G-dly soul, each one of us can also be expected to live up to these standards."[1]

This is reflected in the words of the Alter Rebbe:[2] "Every Jew possesses within him a spark of Moshe our Teacher." Thus one should never feel that a lofty level of refinement and G-dly service is beyond his reach and expectations. Just as our great *tzaddikim*

---

1. *Likkutei Sichos*, vol. 15, p. 130.
2. *Tanya*, ch. 42.

and chassidim lived up to certain levels and achievements, so can we, commensurate with our level.

In my work as a rabbinic chaplain, I have found that the biggest obstacle to a person's spiritual growth and peace of mind is worry and anxiety. Not only does this prevent people from living joyfully in the present, but it can actually interfere with the flow of Divine blessings destined for them. The wisdom of Torah and *Chassidus* teaches us that the more one can remove worry from his life, the more he becomes a vessel for these blessings.

This is alluded to in the Hebrew term for worry, *d'agah*, דאגה. The word consists of four of the first five letters of the Hebrew alphabet (**alef**, *beis*, **gimmel, dalet, hei**). Why is the letter *beis* missing? The letter *beis* stands for ברכה, "blessing," and בטחון, "trust." Where worry resides, blessing and trust do not dwell.

The antidote to our worries has been prescribed to us by our Sages, who teach that having a positive outlook toward life's challenges actually helps bring about a positive outcome. This is illustrated in the *Talmud* by Rabbi Nachum Ish Gamzu whose unwavering belief in his adage "*Gam zu letovah* — This too is for the good" miraculously transformed the potential tragedies in his life to good. In more recent times, the Tzemach Tzedek, the third Rebbe of Chabad, encouraged us to "*Tracht gut vet zain gut* — Think good and it will be good*" as a real solution to our difficulties and challenges.

May we merit that our belief and trust in G-d and our assiduous efforts in personal refinement will usher in the immediate Redemption with *Mashiach*, our righteous redeemer.

Rabbi Dovid Shraga Polter

Oak Park, Michigan
Yud Shvat, 5764 (2004)

DEDICATION

והבוטח בה׳ חסד יסובבנו

"But he who trusts in the L-rd
is surrounded by kindness"

Psalms 32:10

This book is dedicated to my dear father

הרב משה ירחמיאל בן רייזל שיחי׳

who teaches and inspires by his sheer presence
and who personifies *ahavas haTorah v'ahavas hachayim,*
love for Torah and love for life.
May the merit of all those whose hearts he has ignited
stand him in good stead and lead him, *b'ezras HaShem,*
to a complete and speedy recovery.

ACKNOWLEDGMENTS

I offer my humble gratitude to the One Above for granting me the merit to use His teachings in the hope of inspiring others — and to my Rebbe, Rabbi Menachem Mendel Schneerson, who continues to inspire me and drive me beyond that which I could ever accomplish on my own.

My warmest thanks go to the entire staff of my publisher, Sichos In English. To my editor, Rochel Chana Schilder, for her unending patience and meticulous editorial assistance, especially for providing continuous insight and encouragement in a complex undertaking. To Rabbi Arel'e Raskin for his erudite expertise, Yosef Yitzchok Turner for his skillful preparation of the manuscript for publication, and Rabbi Yonah Avtzon for his overall coordination and tireless involvement in seeing the final product come to fruition.

To my colleagues in Oak Park, Rabbi Moshe Zaklikofsky and Rabbi Yosef Yitzchok Gourarie, for their invaluable assistance. To my *chaver*, Dr. Baruch Silverstein, for his professional advice in meeting standards of achievement.

To my beloved parents, Rabbi & Mrs. Moshe Yerachmiel Polter, whose devotion to their children's education is a model of commitment to Jewish values. And to my parents-in-law, Rabbi and Mrs. Azriel Schanowicz, whose righteous example of living a Torah lifestyle I value and admire. Lastly, my wife, Rochel, whose *binah yeseirah* (added measure of wisdom) contributes volumes to our home and family, serving as the support for our family. May Hashem grant us the strength to continue to share and care. Together may we enjoy further *nachas* from our children, may they live long and healthy years. And to our children, for challenging me in the quest of Torah knowledge. They are the impetus that drives me to search for more meaningful answers.

INTRODUCTION

THE ORIGINS OF SELF-EXAMINATION

When Rabbi Shneur Zalman of Liadi,[1] the first Rebbe of the Chabad chassidic movement, was imprisoned in Petersburg for subversive activity against the Czar, he was visited by the chief investigator. "How is it," he asked Rabbi Shneur Zalman, "that the G-d in your Torah asked Adam, the first man, '*Ayeka* — Where are you?' Surely G-d knew where he was!"

Rabbi Shneur Zalman responded: "'*Ayeka* — Where are you?' is G-d's call to every person on earth, asking, 'Where do you stand?' A person has been given so many days and so many years on earth, and he must constantly ask himself what he has accomplished in those years and how much good he has contributed to the world."[2]

From the creation of human life close to six thousand years ago, man has been asking himself the same question: "*Ayeka*: What's the right way to behave? Am I on the right path? Have I

---

1. Known throughout this book as the "Alter Rebbe." His successors are known by the names: the Mitteler Rebbe, the Tzemach Tzedek, the Rebbe Maharash, the Rebbe Rashab, the Rebbe Rayatz (also known as the Previous Rebbe) and "the Rebbe" (see footnote 11). The teachings of the Chabad branch of Chassidism are the most prolific and most widely known of the chassidic schools of thought, and are the basis for most of the stories and teachings in this book.
2. *Rabbi Schneur Zalman of Liadi, A Biography*, Nissan Mindel, Kehot Publication Society, NY, 1969.

acted correctly? How can I rectify my flaws and shortcomings? How can I find peace?"

In various stages of history, society has provided man with the means of self-rectification. On an external level, laws and court systems were instituted to keep man's more primal and selfish instincts in check. In agricultural and industrial societies, involvement in back-breaking manual labor prevented man from engaging in much more than the struggle to secure his physical needs. More recently, a preponderance of leisure time, the lack of political oppression, and the explosion of self-help/psychological modalities have provided people with the means and the environment to explore their inner psyches in an attempt to find moral guidance and true peace.

THE DIVINE ROAD TO SELF-AWARENESS

Like everything in life, that which is man-made is prone to the flaws and limitations of the human condition. Various schools of psychological thought have peaked and waned in the last few hundred years, flowing from one ideology to another in an attempt to create sense and stability in a seemingly irrational world. One generation may tout leniency in child-rearing; another, military strictness. One generation may promote puritanism and the restraint of one's bodily drives; another may encourage indulgence. The inconsistency in these methods of guidance is not intrinsically bad, it's just not the truth: anything true by its very nature is eternal and unchangeable.

Torah and its *mitzvos*, rooted as they are in their Divine source, are the only constant in an ever-changing world. The unfolding of G-dly wisdom — from the Five Books of Moses, to the "Oral Law" of the *Talmud*, to the *Kabbalah* and the inner spiritual dimensions of chassidic teachings — has provided man with Divinely inspired answers to the moral, spiritual, and existential questions that have plagued him from the beginning of time.

THE ADVENT OF CHASSIDUS

The mid-1600s marked one of the darkest periods in Jewish history. Two major events threatened the physical and spiritual survival of the Jewish people: the crippling Cossack persecutions of Jews in Poland, Ukraine and White Russia led by the demonic Bogdan Chmielnicki, and the spiritual chaos that followed the exposure of messianic hopeful Shabtai Zvi as a fraud and *apikores* (heretic).[3]

Against this backdrop of havoc and despair, the great chassidic master, the holy Baal Shem Tov,[4] introduced the remedy for the ills of the Jewish nation by revealing a body of Torah wisdom known as *Chassidus*, the mystical dimension of the Torah. The revelation of these teachings — encompassing philosophical insights, the mystical secrets of Creation, psychology, and a down-to-earth guide for refining one's social and personal behavior — provided the spiritual "smelling salts" for the collective "faint" of the Jewish nation.[5]

---

3. See *On the Essence of Chassidus*, Rabbi Menachem M. Schneerson, Kehot Publication Society, Brooklyn, NY, 1978; 1986, p. 2.
4. Lit., "The Master of the Good Name," Rabbi Yisrael ben Eliezer, 1698-1760.
5. The Sages tell us that when a person faints, he is revived by the sound of his name whispered in his ear, as a person's (Hebrew) name has an essential connection to his general life-force. The teachings of the Baal Shem Tov (whose first name was Israel) were like a rejuvenating voice whispering in the ear of the Children of Israel. (See *Kesser Shem Tov*, 1998 edition, p. 228; *Likkutei Sichos*, vol. 2, p. 516.)

Little by little, the promulgation of chassidic teachings revitalized the spirits of the Jewish people and put them back on their feet. In addition to providing them with a profound intellectual wellspring of Divine wisdom, *Chassidus* guided and inspired their spiritual reawakening and healing. And these same teachings, shaped and disseminated by the Baal Shem Tov's successor, the Maggid of Mezritch, and the chassidic Rebbeim who followed, are as much an antidote for the spiritual ills of today as they were then.

The Talmudic Sages tell us that "G-d always provides the cure before the affliction."[6] In the Baal Shem Tov's times, chassidic teachings provided the remedy for the ailing soul of the Jewish people; so too in our times, *Chassidus* has the power to heal all the spiritual plagues we now face.[7]

We are currently witnessing an unprecedented search for meaning and moral guidance, as the Psalmist says: *"This* is the generation of those who search for Him."[8] Fed up with greed, the superficiality of western culture, and the turmoil of world events, people are turning to G-d for comfort and meaning. Psychology and self-help teachings, while helpful to an extent, have not provided adequate solutions for issues such as existential doubt, spiritual struggles, and the ability to face life's daily challenges with equanimity. The teachings of *Chassidus*, if followed as prescribed, can bring about lasting and positive transformation in all areas of one's life.

---

6. *Megillah* 13b.
7. *Kitzurim VeHe'aros LeSefer Likkutei Amarim*, p. 125. See fn. 16.
8. *Tehillim* 24:6.

For time-tested spiritual and emotional healing, chassidim have always looked to stories about, or advice from, *tzaddikim* — righteous people whose entire being is bound up with G-dliness. People are born with two inclinations — an inclination toward selfish bodily drives and a transcendent drive toward Divinity — and they spend their lives engaged in the battle between them. But in every generation there exists a small number of *tzaddikim*, holy people who are motivated by their G-dly soul alone,[9] and we look to their behavior as the quintessential example of how best to live our lives. With his only desire to fulfill the will of the Creator, the *tzaddik* is an earthly representation of human perfection. Although a real person of flesh and blood, he is our earthly metaphor of how G-d behaves and wants us to behave.[10]

The chassidic story usually presents a common scenario or dilemma in which a *tzaddik*, or one of his disciples, demonstrates an exemplary mode of behavior, either personally or through his advice to others. Moreover, although colorful stories such as those presented here are often deceptively simple, they embody profound universal messages. They bring to life many of the deepest teachings of *Chassidus*, elucidating abstract or philosophical concepts in a format one can easily absorb.

The ease with which a listener can involve his heart and soul in the characters and situations of a story is probably the secret of

---

9. See *Tanya*, chs. 1, 10. In addition, there is one *tzaddik*, a Rebbe, a comprehensive soul, who is the head of the entire Jewish people.
10. On the verse (*Devarim* 11:22): "If you will... walk in all His ways and cleave to Him," *Rashi*, the foremost commentator on the Torah, comments: How is it possible to cleave to G-d (given that He is "a consuming fire")? By cleaving to His disciples and to the wise (i.e., *tzaddikim*). As such, we are credited with cleaving to G-d Himself. (See *Kesubos* 111b.)

its impact. Identifying with the predicament challenging each character, the listener considers the choices made by the *tzaddik* in the story and anxiously seeks to anticipate the solution he proposes. In the same way, as we today read — or experience on video — the advice and guidance offered by the Rebbe[11] to men and women in thousands of life's situations, we can learn to emulate his attitudes on life by allowing this advice and guidance to inspire our own decision-making.

The profundity of a chassidic story was plumbed by the founder of Chabad *Chassidus*, Rabbi Shneur Zalman of Liadi, when he said: "When we used to hear a teaching from our mentor, the Maggid of Mezritch, we saw this as the Oral Torah, but when we heard a story from his lips, this was our *Written* Torah."[12]

Not all lessons are learned through stories. A chassidic teaching is often distilled in a chassidic *vort*[13] — a brief and quotable teaching of a Rebbe or chassid of renown, perhaps first given as advice to an individual or as the practical application of a Torah passage. Characteristic of such teachings is their extraordinary ability to identify and resolve a moral, spiritual or psychological dilemma. Above all, they provide guidance for the positive transformation of one's character traits.

HOW TO USE THIS BOOK

Each chassidic story or *vort* in this book was named according to the spiritual or emotional issue it addresses. In truth, many

---

11. The seventh Lubavitcher Rebbe, Rabbi Menachem Mendel Schneerson, known throughout this book as simply "the Rebbe."
12. *Likkutei Dibburim* (English trans.: Kehot Publication Society, Brooklyn, NY, 1987), vol. 1, p. 208.
13. From the Yiddish, literally, "a word."

lessons and teachings can be derived from one story; any attempt to capture its essence and depth in one word is limiting at best. To derive the maximum benefit from a chassidic teaching, the reader must contemplate its details, engage in inner work to find where he and the story resonate, and discover how the resultant insight can enhance and transform his life.

In other words, if *Chassidus* is to be effective as a spiritual remedy, *hisbonenus* is necessary. *Hisbonenus* is literally translated as meditation, but it is more than that. *Hisbonenus* is the process of focusing one's mind on an intellectual concept for a long period of time — contemplating, concentrating, musing, applying — until an insight or revelation is born. Thus, it is not a "quick fix" or easy task. Quick and easy answers are more a product of today's "instant gratification" generation. They may satisfy momentarily, but rarely penetrate a person's whole being. The first stage of *hisbonenus* is stimulation of the mind. With increased concentration, the enlightenment that is awakened then trickles down into the heart and arouses an emotive response — such as a love of G-d or a love of one's fellow Jew — that will ultimately spark an actual change in one's attitudes and daily conduct. It is this application of *Chassidus* that is so effective in refining and healing the person in his totality.

To put it candidly, to benefit from a chassidic story or *vort* you must work. Most stories will undoubtedly evoke questions, or even confusion: "What's the point?" "What did he mean by that?" "What's going on here?" But it is precisely in the contemplation of the answers that the transformation takes place. Someone else's explanations may lend you temporary intellectual closure, but without your own *hisbonenus*, the opportunity for reaping the reward of lasting change is lost.

If you are feeling confusion or emotional discomfort in some area of your life, browse through the Table of Contents until you find a topic that jumps out at you. Turn to that story or *vort* and read it slowly a few times. Contemplate the details and live with them for a day, a week (sometimes a lifetime). Don't skip over phrases you don't understand; ponder them until you feel you've grasped their meaning. Take a notebook and jot down some personal responses to the story, or write freely on whatever thoughts emerge from your subconscious. Note the connections between the passage and your situation. How has the story or the advice helped you understand or rethink your emotional state? How can its lesson heal your dilemma?

Of course you can also just read through the book to gain a broad awareness of chassidic responses to various life issues.

FARBRENGEN AND MASHPIA:
A MODEL FOR GROUP AND INDIVIDUAL GUIDANCE

You may have done *hisbonenus* and all the above exercises, but some allusions in the story may still be too obscure or cryptic to figure out on your own. Or you may be in denial about some untoward aspect of your character and will not allow yourself to resonate with the story or derive benefit from it. In the latter case, it is helpful to find others to act as a mirror, to provide an unthreatening and loving nudge into areas of your psyche you have been reluctant or too afraid to enter.

In the chassidic lifestyle there is a variety of established methods for obtaining help and support for one's personal growth. One is the chassidic *farbrengen*, a gathering of like-minded individuals who have come together to share their thoughts and struggles in life and gain inspiration from one another in a setting of friendship, spontaneity, and nonjudgmental criticism. Another is the kind of *farbrengen* that is led by a *mashpia.* This spiritual mentor is a chassid who is well-soaked in chassidic teachings and chassidic lore, and who has been seasoned and sensitized by his own self-critical responses to life's challenges.

Whether those present at a *farbrengen* participate by speaking or by listening, their common goal is to refine their own conduct and to improve their spiritual health. Focus is often given to the importance of designating fixed times for Torah study and applying its principles to self-improvement. At unscheduled interludes, the group allows the singing of a meditative chassidic melody to express the inexpressible yearnings of the soul.

But the heart of a chassidic *farbrengen* is the story. In this warm setting, the analysis of the story is no mere intellectual exercise. The group leader evaluates the needs and level of the participants and judiciously selects and interprets various chassidic stories to evoke self-revelation and self-correction in the listeners. Through the ensuing discussion and personal interaction, participants of a *farbrengen* are more willing to relax their grip on the protective armor that keeps them safe but perpetually stuck. How such a gathering can penetrate even a heart of stone!

Another — and indispensable — tool for personal growth is one-on-one interaction with a *mashpia* who is able to objectively evaluate an individual's progress in his overall service of G-d.[14]

---

14. This is illustrated in the *mishnah*: "Acquire for yourself a Rav (a mentor)..." (*Ethics of the Fathers* 1:6). The importance of this fundamental requirement has been discussed in great detail by the Rebbe (*Hisvaaduyos 5746*, vol. 4, p. 173; see also "Provide Yourself a Teacher," *Sichos In English*, vol. 32, p. 44ff.).

When the kind of *mashpia* described above is told of a particular problem or behavior flaw, he can help draft an individual strategy for self-awareness and self-examination. Guidance is given with the utmost delicacy, and a story is often used to illustrate how to rectify the particular flaw that needs correction. The impersonal nature of the story allows the *mekabel* (lit., "the recipient") to assimilate the message without feeling defensive or threatened by a more direct approach.

The importance of recognizing and admitting one's spiritual weaknesses is illustrated by a passage from a book of teachings compiled by the Rebbe.[15]

The early sages ... determined that the healing of the soul is like the healing of the body:[16]

[In both cases,] it is first critical to identify the location of the illness, whether it is caused by the crassness, grossness and corruption of one's physical body or by a failing in his soul-powers — the person being inclined to undesirable traits like arrogance or falsehood and the like. Or, the source of the malady may be habit — inadequate upbringing or unwholesome environment having brought on bad habits.

Without ascertaining the specific site of the illness and the cause of infection, it is impossible to embark on a cure. One can only prescribe an [overall program of] proper conduct in all matters, [i.e.,] what to do and what to avoid: to "do good" in terms of observing *mitzvos*, designating times for Torah-

---

15. *HaYom Yom*, entry for 16 Sivan; excerpted from a long letter of the Previous Rebbe (*Igros Kodesh of the Rebbe Rayatz*, vol. 4, p. 352).
16. See *Sefer HaSichos 5708*, p. 264, which states, "Just as there are medicines for physical illnesses, so, too, there are remedies for the maladies of the soul."

study, and acquiring good character traits; and also to "turn away from evil."

Most urgent of all, however, is that the patient make himself aware of two things: a) to know that he is ill and desire most fervently to be cured of his malady; and b) to know that he *can* be cured, with the hope and absolute trust that, with G-d's help, he *will* indeed be cured of his sickness.

If one seeks to clear his heart of unwanted burdens and struggles — not by escaping them but by working through them — he will discuss them with a *mashpia* who can create an environment of empathy in which problems can be aired and counsel can be offered. Indeed, opening up to another will enable one to derive the fullest benefit from the stories and teachings presented in this book.

THE
STORIES

ACCEPTANCE

It says in *Ethics of the Fathers* (1:12): "Be of the disciples of Aharon... loving the created beings, and bringing them close to the Torah."

The term "created beings" may seem an archaic or awkward translation of the Hebrew, but its usage is actually intentional and precise. By using "created beings" instead of "people," the verse implies that Aharon would reach out to individuals whose only redeeming virtue was the fact that they were G-d's creations.

The lesson for us is to always remember that one's quintessential love for another Jew should not be contingent on any exterior quality such as talent, beauty, or intellect. Rather one should accept and love a friend just because of his innate virtue of having been chosen by G-d to be created. This alone is sufficient reason to love and respect another.

Sichos Kodesh, Acharon Shel Pesach, 5736
Sichos Kodesh, Matos-Masei, 5737

True

ACCOMPLISHMENTS

When one speaks about "serving G-d with truth," this does not imply — as some erroneously think — that one must pulverize mountains and shatter boulders, or turn the world upside down. The absolute truth is that any act performed in the service of G-d, whatever it may be, is perfectly satisfactory when executed with a sincere intent: a *berachah* (blessing) pronounced with heartfelt intention; a word of prayer expressed with a prepared heart and an awareness of "before Whom you stand"; a passage in the Torah said with the understanding that it is the word of G-d; a verse of *Tehillim*; a beneficent character trait expressed in befriending another with affection and love.

HaYom Yom, entry for 2 Adar I

The Value of

ACTION

Groaning in and of itself won't do a bit of good. A groan is only a key to open the heart and eyes, so that one does not sit with folded arms, but plans orderly work and activity — each person wherever he can be effective — to campaign for bolstering Torah, spreading Torah and the observance of *mitzvos*. One person might do this through his writing, another with speaking, another with his wealth.

HaYom Yom, entry for 23 Teves

The Value of

ACTION(2)

The Baal Shem Tov was once in need of financial assistance and approached the home of someone from whom he was hoping to gain some support. He knocked on the man's door but left immediately before the homeowner could answer. Seeing the Baal Shem Tov in the distance, the homeowner chased after him and, after ascertaining the reason for his visit, offered him his needs. He asked, "If you needed me so much, why did you just knock and leave?"

The Baal Shem Tov replied: "In truth, sustenance comes from G-d. However, there is a verse in the Torah that states: '...and G-d will bless you in all that you *do*.' Thus in order to fulfill the directive 'in all that you do,' I just needed to perform an action such as knocking on the door. Once I had done my part, I was sure that G-d would do His."

The lesson to be learned is this: One must trust that his sustenance comes only from G-d, and that all man's exertion in sustaining himself is nothing more than a vessel in which G-d desires and is able to bestow His blessing.

Sichos Kodesh, Devarim, 5734

Accepting

ADVICE

During a private audience with the Previous Rebbe, a lumber merchant shared his business concerns with the Rebbe. The Rebbe's advice to him was to be more careful in the performance of *mitzvos*. The merchant responded unenthusiastically to the Rebbe's suggestions, as he had hoped instead to receive practical business advice.

In surprise, the Rebbe reacted: "You surely agree that I am a greater expert in matters relating to Judaism and Torah than I am in the area of lumber. It is well known to all that I have dedicated my life to the ways of Torah and *mitzvos* and Jewish living, as did my parents and grandparents. Still, you are confident in consulting me about an area in which I do *not* specialize—and—you would gladly accept my directives.

"In the area of my expertise, however — Torah and *mitzvos* — you don't bother asking my advice. Furthermore, you appear uninterested when I explain to you the physical and spiritual benefits [of performing *mitzvos* carefully]."

Igros Kodesh of the Rebbe, vol. 13, p. 195

ANGER

The Previous Rebbe related in the name of his uncle, Reb Zalman Aharon (the older brother of the Rebbe Rashab):

"When one becomes angry, he should wait at least sixty-one minutes, and then he can think clearly."

Igros Kodesh of the Rebbe, vol. 7, p. 116

Our Sages of blessed memory taught: "Whoever is in a rage resembles an idolater."

The reason for this is that when a person is angry, faith in G-d and in G-d's individual Divine Providence have left him. For were he to believe that what happened to him was G-d's doing, he would not be angry at all. True, the person who is cursing him, or striking him, or causing damage to his property is doing so out of free choice and is therefore guilty of his evil choice according to the laws of man and the laws of Heaven. Additionally, the perpetrator of the offense cannot plead innocence on the grounds that he is merely an instrument in the hands of Divine Providence. Nevertheless, regarding the person harmed, this incident was already decreed in Heaven, and "G-d has many agents" through which He can act.

Tanya, Iggeres HaKodesh, Epistle 25

The Positive Side of

ARROGANCE

There was a chassid of the Alter Rebbe, Reb Mordechai Liepler, who claimed that his arrogance was responsible for making him a chassid.

To explain: When the *yetzer hara* (negative inclination) would confront him and say: "Mottel, commit a sin," he would face it resolutely and respond: "I am a chassid of the Alter Rebbe, not to mention I am wealthy and learned — and *you* are attempting to convince *me* to transgress?!"

Toras Menachem 5715, vol. 1, p. 58

The Mitteler Rebbe once told someone to become an "onion."

This person had been traveling from town to town spreading chassidic teachings but had recently decided to stop. All the fuss over him and his talents, he claimed, had been feeding his ego. Now he had to work on himself to diminish that negative aspect of his character.

The Mitteler Rebbe showed no pity. "An onion should become of you," he exclaimed, "but teach others what you must teach them!"

Why an onion?

An onion is added to the pot not to be eaten, but only to give flavor to the chicken and the broth. Like the onion, you sometimes need to sacrifice your own personal growth so others may grow.

Toras Menachem 5715, vol. 1, p. 313ff.
Sichos Kodesh, Rosh Chodesh Adar 5740

Faulty
ASSUMPTIONS

Once when the chassid Reb Monya Monoson had a private audience with the Rebbe Rashab, their discussion concerned several simple individuals whom the Rebbe praised. This surprised Reb Monya and he asked the Rebbe, "What's the big deal [about them]?" The Rebbe responded, "They possess special qualities" to which Reb Monya replied, "I don't see it."

As was known, Reb Monya was a successful diamond merchant. When the Rebbe asked him whether he had a pouch of diamonds with him, he responded affirmatively. "However," he said, "due to the lack of sunshine, it would not be advisable to examine them presently." Later, Reb Monya took the pouch into a second room and displayed the diamonds, pointing out the incredible quality of one specific stone. The Rebbe remarked, "I don't see anything special in it," to which Reb Monya replied, "[For that,] one must be a *maven* (expert)."

The Rebbe then told him, "When it comes to seeing the special qualities of a Jew's soul, one also has to be a *maven*."

Sefer HaSichos 5705, p. 41

ATTENTIVENESS

The Mitteler Rebbe (who lived in the same house as his father, the Alter Rebbe) was once sitting in his room deeply engrossed in Torah study while, in the same room, his youngest child slept quietly in a crib. Suddenly, the baby rolled out of his crib onto the floor and began crying loudly. So immersed in contemplation was the Mitteler Rebbe that he did not hear anything and he continued his studies.

The Alter Rebbe was sitting in his room, farther away from the baby's room. Although he was also immersed in study, he nonetheless heard the baby crying. He entered the room and put the baby back in the crib. After he had rocked the baby back to sleep, he returned to his room. A while later, the Alter Rebbe rebuked his son and said: "One must never be so immersed in his studies that he does not hear the cry of a child."

Toras Menachem 5714, vol. 1, p. 229ff.

ATTITUDE

A chassid, stricken with troubles, once approached the Maggid of Mezritch for counsel. Realizing the desperation of the chassid, the Maggid referred him to Reb Zusia of Anipoli to further guide him in dealing with his struggles.

Reb Zusia was himself impoverished and faced severe personal struggles. However, he was known for his joyful and cheerful attitude in spite of his conditions.

When the chassid reached Reb Zusia, he was greatly surprised to find him in such an uplifted mood. He realized that it was unnecessary to express the reason for his coming, since he immediately understood the obvious meaning of the Maggid's intention in sending him there.

Sichos Kodesh, Va'eira, 5729

ATTITUDE (2)

Once, the Baal Shem Tov (the *Besht*) told his students to harness the horses for a journey together. Shortly after they set off, the *Besht* instructed the driver to stop the horses, whereupon he and his students descended from the wagon. They met an old person carrying two buckets of water, and when the *Besht* inquired as to his well-being, the person responded with a broken heart: "I am old, yet I must continue my laborious work. Sometimes, while carrying heavy loads of water, I stumble on a stone and the water comes pouring out of the buckets, which forces me to return and refill them. I have children, thank G-d, but they just don't have the time to spend with me." He concluded with a sigh, the *Besht* blessed him, and they returned home.

Several weeks later the *Besht* instructed that the horses be harnessed once again for an outing to that same place. He and his students descended and again met this same person. When the *Besht* greeted him and inquired as to his welfare, the person responded with great jubilance: "I earn a livelihood as a water carrier, thank G-d. Although I am old and stumble at times, causing the water to spill out of the buckets, thank G-d I am able to return and refill them. I have children, thank G-d, and although they are busy, I am grateful for even the small amount of time that they are able to help me."

The *Besht* explained to his students:

Our Sages teach that "Man is judged from Above each and every day," and elsewhere it is stated that "Man is judged on Rosh HaShanah for the entire year." How do we reconcile the two statements?

There is a verdict that is established on Rosh HaShanah regarding how much one will earn for the year. In addition there is a verdict as to how and in what fashion one will receive his portion, whether sadly and out of anger, or with a cheerful countenance. This verdict is established each and every day [and is dependent on our merits]. Thus we found the man responding in two different ways.*

Otzar Sippurei Chabad, vol. 14, p. 139

---

* Like the bestowal of one's material needs, a person's attitude toward his situation in life is also a blessing from Above, and is determined by the person's merits.

The Proper

ATTITUDE (3)

There is no one for whom to pride oneself, [meaning, is there any room for arrogance in Divine service?]. We must toil strenuously. With patience and friendliness we can prevail in all things, with G-d's help. With a denigrating attitude toward others and an inflation of our own importance, we lose everything, G-d forbid.

HaYom Yom, entry for 20 Iyar

AWAKENING THE
JEWISH SPARK;
The "Pintele Yid"

The Previous Rebbe once related that when bombs would drop on Warsaw during WWII, all the Jews would go into hiding. Once, a whole group gathered in one room: the Rebbe, average people, simple people, and those who considered themselves to be completely disconnected from Judaism. When a bomb blew up nearby, they all yelled out in unison: "*Shema Yisrael* (Hear O Israel...)."

The reason for this was that it stemmed from the deepest level of their soul, the *yechidah*. And although their proximity to the Rebbe would only explain what awakened them to yell, the actual yelling of the *Shema* came from their own *yechidah*.

Likkutei Sichos, vol. 2, p. 334

Jewish Roots — A Sense of

BELONGING

George Rohr is a businessman who has been inspired by the Rebbe, and who supports many Lubavitch activities. Once, before Yom Kippur, when receiving *lekach* (honey cake) from the Rebbe, it occurred to him that he should give something to the Rebbe and not merely take from him. With that thought in mind, he told the Rebbe that for Rosh HaShanah, he had organized a *minyan* for over 130 Jews who had no Jewish background.

The Rebbe immediately became serious. "With no Jewish background?" he repeated, looking at Mr. Rohr intently.

Not understanding what he had said wrong, Mr. Rohr could only say again, "With no background."

"Go back and tell them," the Rebbe said, "that they have a Jewish background! They have the background of Avraham, Yitzchak and Yaakov."

From To Know and To Care, vol. 2, p. 75

BRAVERY

On one of the occasions that the Previous Rebbe was being interrogated by the Communist authorities, his examiner brandished a gun with bravado. "This little toy has made stronger men than you talk," he told the Rebbe.

"That toy is only effective," the Rebbe replied, "against a man who has one world and many gods. I, however, have one G-d and two worlds."*

Likkutei Sichos, vol. 3, p. 806

---

* The Previous Rebbe was referring to the physical world and the spiritual world known as the World to Come, the abode of worthy souls that are not enclothed in a physical body.

The Benefit of a

BROKEN HEART

A deeply troubled Jew decided to visit the Rebbe Rashab in hope of finding some solace. His condition was dire and warranted much help, but the Rebbe declined from offering assistance saying, "There is not much I can do at this time."

Upon hearing this, the Jew left the room brokenheartedly and burst out in tears. In the midst of his sobs, he happened to cross paths with Reb Zalman Aharon (the *RaZa*), the Rebbe's brother, and in great anguish related his astonishing experience with the Rebbe to him.

Baffled by the man's experience, the *RaZa* resolved at once to approach his brother the Rebbe and ask him for an explanation of his seeming lack of compassion for this man's painful request. When he met with the Rebbe, he informed him how great this man's disappointment was at the Rebbe's unexpected response to him.

The Rebbe's countenance changed. He immediately donned his *gartel* and asked that the Jew be summoned. As soon as he stepped foot into the Rebbe's study, the Rebbe granted his blessing and shortly afterwards, the man's condition began to improve.

The radical change came about because the Rebbe saw that the man's brokenheartedness had fundamentally changed him. Originally, the Jew was not a fitting vessel for G-d's benevolence, but when the man examined himself with a broken heart, he became worthy of the blessing.

Likkutei Sichos, vol. 15, p. 126

CHALLENGE

It was at a festive *Rosh Chodesh* meal that the students of the holy Baal Shem Tov discerned that their master was in an unusually bland mood. They attempted to arouse joy in him but to no avail.

Suddenly, in the midst of the festivity, a villager by the name of Reb Dovid arrived. As soon as he entered, the *Besht* began to show signs of joy and elation. He then honored the villager with reverence and a place to sit at his side.

The *Besht's* extreme behavior aroused much curiosity among his students, and they were eager for an explanation.

Sensing their wonderment, the *Besht* sent Reb Dovid on an assignment [so that the *Besht* could explain his actions to the chassidim]. He then related to the chassidim that Reb Dovid was accustomed to saving every penny of his hard-earned income in order to purchase the most beautiful *esrog** possible. He would wait all year long and travel long distances in order to obtain an *esrog* of the highest quality.

Since he and his family were impoverished, his wife resented his spending all that time and money on his *esrog*, as she felt his priorities lay with meeting the material needs of the family. When he finally arrived home with his well-invested *esrog*, his wife was

---

* A citron used in the *mitzvah* of the Four Species during the Sukkos holiday.

overcome with such great frustration that she broke off the *esrog*'s *pitom* (tip) — making it unfit for use.

Calmly he reacted: "She is most probably correct, for I must not be worthy of such an *esrog*. After all, how does this come to a simpleton like me?"

The holiday moments were nearing and Reb Dovid was resigned to join in with the other villagers in using the communal *esrog*. However, he still desired to be an owner of an *esrog* so that he could fulfill the *mitzvah* of "you should take for yourself" (i.e., possess your own). Seeing that he had no money and did not want to borrow on collateral, he took an object from his home and brought it to a dealer to be exchanged for cash. With the money, he joined in the ownership of the community *esrog*. The *Besht* concluded: Ever since the historical moment of the binding of Yitzchak, no one has been tested on such a magnitude. For this reason I have honored him, and in turn he has evoked within me great joy.

Sefer HaSichos 5696, p. 148

CHANGE

Once, when a wealthy chassid came to the Rebbe [Rashab], the Rebbe mentioned the Talmudic passage: "The world is a turning wheel," and added that although a wheel is round, there is still a top and a bottom.

The Rebbe continued: In the central garden of Vienna there is a large Ferris wheel that stands above the ground. On its sides hang wagons made of glass and decorated with metal trimmings so that the one riding is able to see from all angles. When the wagon is lifted off the ground, he is also lifted. And when he reaches the highest point, he is able to see very far. The wheel turns and the wagons begin to descend, and in this way the turning of the wheel brings about the ascent and descent of the wagons.

There is a time when the person is on top, and there is a time when the person is on the bottom.

The nature of man is that when he is on top, he feels uplifted and laughs out of goodness, and when he is, G-d forbid, on the bottom, he is saddened and weeps out of bitterness and a heavy heart.

However, both of these people are fools.

The one on the bottom who is weeping out of sadness must be challenged: Why are you crying? It is only a wheel, and a wheel's nature is to turn. G-d will help and you will be helped.

And the one on top of the wheel who feels exalted must also be challenged: Why are you so excited? It is only a wheel and a wheel's nature is to turn.

Sefer HaSichos 5696, p. 32;
Igros Kodesh of the Rebbe Rayatz, vol. 5, p. 117

CHILD-REARING

A caring father loves his children. The father is pained when the child is lacking something; his entire goal is to see to it that all of his child's needs are met.

Even when the child behaves improperly, his father does not hit him. He knows that a smack will not accomplish anything. He knows that his child is not to be blamed; rather his surroundings and undesirable friends are the main cause for his unkind behavior.

His father takes his son aside and says to him: Why do you compare yourself to them? After all, they are hooligans who roam the streets and tear off an apple and eat it without making a blessing. You, on the other hand, go to *cheder*, wear *tzitzis*, and make blessings. When, with G-d's help, you will become *bar mitzvah*, you will be eligible to complete a *minyan*. Nine Jews will be waiting for you in *shul* and will not be allowed to recite certain prayers without you as the number ten. It is the greatest act that you can do. With these words the father lifts up his child and empowers him to improve his behavior.

Sefer HaSichos 5709, p. 309

CHOICES

The Rogatchover Gaon once related that the most difficult day of the week for him was Shabbos. During the week, when great waves of thoughts and insights flooded his mind, he always had the opportunity to write them down. Putting something in writing confines one's stream of thoughts, making it easier to come to a conclusion regarding the issue at hand. As he was not able to do this on Shabbos, he had to toil greatly in order to reach some type of clarification.

Each and every one of us has the opportunity to choose whether material burdens such as earning a livelihood should dominate our lives (in which case our thoughts rob us of peace of mind), or whether to exchange this burden and toil for a more spiritual and gratifying burden, the toil of Torah study. In the latter, one toils so much that he is overwhelmed with one insight versus another to the degree that he struggles to resolve the two.

Likkutei Sichos, vol. 1, p. 117

Honoring G-d's

CHOICES

The Rebbe Maharash would say: "If I could have... if I would have... if I was... if only I were.... Statements like this constitute a denial of G-d."

Otzar Pisgamei Chabad, p. 200

COMPASSION

When the Rebbe Rashab was a child of five years old, he was playing with his older brother Reb Zalman Aharon. Since both of them were raised in a home where discussion of the Rebbe-chassid relationship was very common, they decided to play a game of "Rebbe and chassid."

The older brother, Reb Zalman Aharon, played the role of "Rebbe," and the Rashab assumed that of the "chassid."

The *RaZa* sat down on a chair and fixed his hat like that of a Rebbe. The Rashab (playing the part of a chassid) entered the "Rebbe's room" and requested a *tikkun* (rectification) for a particular shortcoming of his. "This past Shabbos," he said, "I ate peanuts. And only after I finished them did I remember that the Alter Rebbe writes in his *Siddur* that one shouldn't eat peanuts on Shabbos."*

Reb Zalman Aharon answered immediately with advice. "Begin praying from a *Siddur*, not by heart. This is your *tikkun*."

The Rashab responded: "You're not acting like a real Rebbe."

The *RaZa* asked, "Why? I gave you good advice."

---

* A person should refrain from eating nuts on Shabbos unless he takes them out of the shell *erev* Shabbos (*Hilchos Rabsa L'Shabbata*, in the *Siddur of the Alter Rebbe*, p. 320).

The Rashab answered: "A Rebbe first lets out a sigh of commiseration — and only then does he give advice. You didn't show me any compassion — and therefore you are not a Rebbe and your advice is useless."

Sichos Kodesh 5720, Purim

COMPETITION

There are two levels in the [refinement of the] *middos* (emotional attributes). The first is *iskafia*, where the emotions obey the dictates of the intellect (in refraining from unwanted behavior). The second is *is'hapcha*, to completely transform the *middos*.

To illustrate: imagine a person has a competitor in his line of business, in the same district. When he allows himself to be controlled by his animal soul, animosity is aroused in him toward his competitor. The intellect of the G-dly soul then comes and says: Certainly you are a believer that G-d is the Master of the universe; therefore, if G-d has ordained for you to earn a livelihood, how can your competitor take it from you, contrary to G-d's will? If, however, it was decided on High that you would earn less income, do you think that the competitor is the only means by which G-d can accomplish this? Therefore, your competitor is taking nothing from you. If so, why should you resent him?

After many internal debates, the person begins to feel that this hatred ceases to affect his actions, then his speech, and finally even his thoughts. However, the person still does not reach the level of *is'hapcha*, transformation.

The G-dly soul continues and says, "You must love your fellow as yourself." After all, you are a specialist in his line of business, and since his success has no effect on yours, help him with some good advice, with a loan, etc., until ultimately, the hatred is transformed to love.

This latter part is the meaning of the loftier level of *is'hapcha*.

Igros Kodesh of the Rebbe, vol. 3, p. 197

CONCENTRATION

Once, while standing on a riverbank next to his timber business near the city of Riga, Reb Binyomin Kletzker (a chassid of the Alter Rebbe) was found deeply immersed in thought, apparently in a deep concept of *Chassidus* that required profound concentration. He stood in the same position for five consecutive hours. When he came back to himself, he was shocked at the bewildered expressions on the faces of several onlookers. He exclaimed: My wonder and bewilderment [towards you] is greater than yours [toward me], for to be thinking about timber in Riga while reciting the *Shema* is considered acceptable! But when one meditates on *Echad* (the unity of G-d) during business... *that* elicits bewilderment!!

Sefer HaSichos 5686, p. 100, and fns. there

Inner

CONFLICT

[When one is plagued by negative thoughts and he subsequently banishes them from his mind...] one should not feel depressed or very troubled at heart. He ought to be *somewhat* troubled by the occurrence of these thoughts, otherwise he may become indifferent to them and will cease to wage war against them. But he ought not to be sorely troubled by them, even if he were to be engaged constantly in this conflict with the thoughts that will always enter his mind. Though he may never rise to the level that precludes their occurrence, he should not be depressed. For perhaps this is what he was created for and this is the service demanded of him — to subdue the *sitra achra* (the side of unholiness) constantly.

Tanya, ch. 27

Eternal

CONNECTION

The *Ramban* (Reb Moshe ben Nachman, known also as Nachmanides) had a student whose name was Reb Avner. Avner rebelled vehemently against his respected teacher and the observance of Judaism. One Yom Kippur he encountered the *Ramban*, who asked him what prompted him to rebel. Avner responded that he once heard the *Ramban* say that everyone and everything in the world, including all the *mitzvos*, were hinted to in the Torah portion of *Haazinu*. Deciding that this was impossible, Avner surmised that all of Judaism must likewise be flawed.

The *Ramban* told him, "I still maintain that what I said is true. Ask me whatever you wish."

In great wonderment, Avner asked, "If it is as you say, then show me where my name Avner is written in the portion."

The *Ramban* quoted the passage *"Amarti afeihem ashbisah mei'enosh zichram* — I thought I would make an end of them; I would eliminate mention of them from mankind," and said, "The third letter of [the last four] words make up the name 'Avner,' with the letter *reish* for 'Reb' as the first one."

Devastated at how gravely mistaken he had been, Avner asked the *Ramban* for a way to rectify all his wrongdoings. The *Ramban* said, "You heard it directly from the Torah": *"Amarti afeihem ashbisah mei'enosh zichram."* Distraught, he embarked on a journey by sea and was never seen again.

What is most intriguing about this story — says the Rebbe — is that his name, as it is hinted to in the Torah, includes the honorable title of Reb, which he merited through his repentance in asking his teacher if there was a remedy for his spiritual decline. And in truth, even before repenting, he carried the title Reb.

Toras Menachem 5742, vol. 1, p. 109

CRISIS

The Previous Rebbe once related to one of his chassidim: It is told about one of the spiritual giants of years gone by that on his cane was engraved the letters *gimmel, zayin,* and *yud,* an acronym for the words "*Gam zeh yaavor* — This too will pass."

When one's fortune turns against him, one should not become downtrodden. Rather he should recognize that all things come from G-d, and further, that this too will pass.

Otzar Pisgamei Chabad, p. 174

How to Give

CRITICISM

A young rabbi once asked the Previous Rebbe for guidance in how to administer rebuke to his congregation. The Rebbe illustrated his answer by describing a sauna. In a sauna, it is customary to slap someone on the back with a towel. An incredible pleasure is derived from these "blows." The harder the smacking, the more pleasure is experienced! However, this is done only when that person's body heat reaches a certain temperature and he sweats profusely.

Just imagine if, the next day, the "slapper" comes along and smacks the other fellow on the back while he's walking down the street. This, of course, would be a most inappropriate time for such treatment, and the person being slapped would be greatly offended.

What is the difference in his reactions? In the sauna, the man was "warmed up" — ready and anticipating a good smack on the back. Out in the cold air, removed from the proper atmosphere and expectation, he is startled and upset. It's the wrong time and place.

In short, to have an effect on another Jew, you must first "warm him up" and make him receptive. Then you can "smack" him (i.e., provide him with guidance through constructive criticism). If you want to help someone with a problem, your intervention has to be at the right time and in the proper setting.

Related by Rabbi Sholom Ber Gordon, 1949

DEPRESSION

When a person finds himself in a situation of "after sunset," when the light of day has given way to gloom and darkness, one must not despair, G-d forbid, but on the contrary, one must fortify oneself with complete trust in G-d, the Essence of Goodness, and take heart in the firm belief that the darkness is only temporary, and it will soon be superseded by a bright light, which will be seen and felt all the more strongly through the supremacy of light over darkness, and by the intensity of the contrast.

... Similarly, with regard to each individual, those who find themselves in a state of personal exile, there is no cause for discouragement and despondence, G-d forbid. On the contrary, one must find increasing strength in complete trust in the Creator and Master of the Universe, that his personal deliverance from distress and confinement is speedily on its way.

A letter from the Rebbe, 15 Kislev 5738 (1978)

It is explained in *Torah Or* (*Parshas Toldos*) that one should utilize depression for the sake of learning assiduously.

Igros Kodesh of the Rebbe, vol. 3, p. 370

The Importance of
EATING

When the Previous Rebbe's grandmother, Rebbetzin Rivkah, was eighteen, she fell ill and the physician ordered her to eat immediately upon awakening. She, however, did not wish to eat before *davening*, so she *davened* very early, then ate breakfast. When her father-in-law, the Tzemach Tzedek, learned of this he said to her: "A Jew must be healthy and strong. Regarding *mitzvos*, the Torah says: 'Live in them,' meaning, one should bring vitality into his performance of the *mitzvos*. To be able to infuse *mitzvos* with vitality, one must be strong and joyful." He then concluded: "You should not be without food. Better to eat for the sake of *davening* than to *daven* for the sake of eating." He then blessed her with long life.

HaYom Yom, entry for 10 Shvat

EDUCATION

"When I was a small child," related the Previous Rebbe, "just after I began to speak, my father, the Rebbe Rashab, told me: 'Whatever you wish to ask, you may ask of me.'

"To guide my education, my father appointed scholarly teachers for me. One of the first things they taught me was to recite the *Modeh Ani* prayer upon awakening by putting one hand opposite the other and bending my head during its recitation.

"As an older child, I remembered my father's invitation to ask him any question, and I asked: 'Why must we put one hand opposite the other and bend the head when reciting *Modeh Ani?*' He responded, 'In truth, we must do without asking why; however I did tell you to ask me your questions....'

"[My father] then asked to summon his eighty-year-old servant Reb Yosef Mordechai and asked him, 'How do you recite *Modeh Ani* in the morning?' He replied, 'I put one hand opposite the other and bend my head.' The Rebbe asked further, 'Why do you do that?' and the servant responded, 'I don't know. When I was a small child I was taught so.'

"'You see,' said my father, the Rebbe, 'he does it because his father taught him to do so, and so it traces back to Moshe and Avraham our Patriarch. And Avraham was the first Jew. One must do without asking why.'

"I then told my father, 'But I am still small.'

"My father answered, 'All Jews are small. And when we grow older, we then begin to see that we are small.'"

Sefer HaMaamarim 5710, p. 244

EFFORT

A chassid once asked the Tzemach Tzedek to bless his son with a good memory so he would remember all that he would see and hear from the Rebbe and chassidim, and therefore be automatically G-d-fearing.

The Rebbe responded: For over fifty years, my grandfather (the Alter Rebbe), my father-in-law (the Mitteler Rebbe) and I have endeavored to teach Jews to "earn" their fear of G-d by their *avodah* (performance of *mitzvos* and study of Torah). Do you want me to deprive your son of this great merit — to become a G-d-fearing Jew by dint of his service to the Creator?

Likkutei Sichos, vol. 3, p. 800; Sefer HaSichos 5700, p. 57

EMPATHY

Sometimes, when the Mitteler Rebbe, and later his son-in-law the Tzemach Tzedek, would have a private audience with people (*yechidus*), they would interrupt the meeting for a period of time and then later continue the *yechidus*. When asked for the reason, each explained: When someone comes for *yechidus* to ask for a *tikkun* (rectification) for a certain matter, I must find a trace of that matter in myself, and only then can I respond. When this person asked me something concerning a very lowly matter, I could not find even a trace of that in myself, so I had to interrupt the *yechidus* [and dig deeper into myself until I could indeed find a trace of it within, and only then could I offer advice].

Likkutei Sichos, vol. 2, p. 382

Channeling

ENTHUSIASM

It is written that a snake's venom is exceedingly hot. This alludes to a condition in which a Jew becomes so wrapped up and roused by the heat of the material world — namely the excitement in the mundane — that his spiritual inspiration is compromised.

Concerning the scorpion it is stated that his venom is cold, connoting a more insidious situation than that of a snake. When one is enthused and excited — albeit in matters relating to the mundane — at least it is a sign of life. He can then channel that enthusiasm to holiness. However, when one is cold and uninspired — a sign of the opposite of life — it is considered far worse.

This will serve to explain the *mishnah*: "If one encounters a snake around his ankle during the *Shemonah Esreh* prayer, he is not to interrupt, whereas when a scorpion is near his ankle he is to interrupt [his prayer] and deal with the impending danger." (*Berachos* 5:1)

When, in the midst of prayer, one is overwhelmed with passion and excitement for worldly things (comparable to the heat of the snake's venom), he is not to interrupt his prayer. Since he possesses the proper tool for spiritual growth, he must merely learn to channel it in a positive way.

On the other hand, when one is besieged during prayer by a sense of coldness and lack of enthusiasm (comparable to the venom of the scorpion), he must interrupt his prayers, since this indicates that his service to G-d is totally inappropriate and must be reconstructed anew.

Likkutei Sichos, vol. 2, p. 374

EQUANIMITY

"*Shivisi* — I have set G-d before me at all times." (*Tehillim* 16:8)

Shivisi is an expression of *hishtavus* (equanimity): no matter what happens, whether people praise or shame you — or with anything else that comes your way — it is all the same to you. This applies likewise to food: whether you are eating delicacies or other things, it is all the same to you. For [with this perspective] the *yetzer hara* is entirely removed from you.

Whatever may happen, say that "it comes from [G-d], blessed be He, and if it is proper in His eyes...." Your motives are altogether for the sake of Heaven, and as for yourself, nothing makes any difference.

This [sense of equanimity] is a very high level.

Tzava'at HaRivash,
The Testament of Rabbi Israel Baal Shem Tov, p. 1

Balancing One's

EXCITEMENT

It was the wedding day of Reb Yaakov Yisrael of Tchirkas and the daughter of the Mitteler Rebbe. The groom's father, Reb Mordechai of Chernobyl, requested that his *mechutan*,* the Mitteler Rebbe, share some words of Torah under the *chuppah* to honor the groom and bride. The Rebbe declined and requested in turn that Reb Mordechai address the assembled family and guests.

The *tzaddik* Reb Mordechai agreed and related the following teaching: "There are three times in a person's life in which great commotions are made: when he is born, when he steps under the *chuppah* [in marriage], and when he is greeted to the World of Truth (i.e., when he passes away)." Continued the *tzaddik*, "It is obvious that in the first and third instances, man does not boast of all the attention and commotion around him. However, when one is at his *chuppah*, he is vulnerable to arrogance from having so many people assembled in his honor. Therefore one must know that this event must be similar in his eyes to the first and third instances, in that he should not become overly excited by all that is happening around him."

---

* The term *mechutan* refers to the relationship between the parents of the bride and groom, who become connected through the marriage of their children.

This lesson is illustrated in *Rashi's* commentary regarding the wedding of our Matriarch Rivkah. On the word *vatiskas* (and she covered herself) (*Bereishis* 24:65), *Rashi* explains that the word is an expression of *vatispa'el* (the reflexive form) as in *vatikaver* (she was buried) and *vatishaver* (it was broken).

The *tzaddik* Reb Mordechai expounded on *Rashi's* commentary and offered a deeper interpretation: *vatispa'el* can also be used for *hispaalus* (excitement), in that Rivka's excitement at the time of her wedding was akin to *vatikaver*, where, in the moment of burial, the excitement is not tainted by any outside impressions. Her excitement, too, was akin to *vatishaver*, as the root of the word *vatishaver* is also applied to the birthing chair (*mishbar*) on which a mother gives birth to her child. Thus *Rashi* is in turn saying: Rivka's *hispaalus* at the time of her wedding was qualitatively the same as the other two phases of her life: *vatikaver* and *vatishaver*. Her excitement was always balanced and was never overly influenced by those who were present at her life-cycle occasions.

Mimayonai HaChassidus Chayei Sarah

EXCUSES

There is a well-known expression relating to excuses:

The word in Hebrew for excuses is אמתלא. If we break the word in the middle, it becomes "אמת לא" meaning "no truth."

Igros Kodesh of the Rebbe, vol. 12, p. 113

FAITH

A chassid once lamented to the Tzemach Tzedek that his faith was unstable and he often had doubts in his beliefs. The Tzemach Tzedek asked him: "What difference does it make to you?" The chassid responded with great emotion, "What do you mean, what difference does it make to me?!!"... The Rebbe then told him, "Your reaction [to my casual remark] indicates that your belief is intact."

Igros Kodesh of the Rebbe, vol. 17, p. 325

FAME

Once, one of the guests at the *Seder* of the Tzemach Tzedek measured his two pieces of matzah to see which was larger.* The Tzemach Tzedek noticed this and commented: "When one must measure (i.e., when one needs to compare) to see that a greater one is indeed greater, it is the smaller one that is really the greater."

The Rebbe Rashab was a small boy at the time. His grandfather's words made a great impression on him, and from that time onward, he would view with displeasure any person whose greatness had to be measured [against someone or something else in order to define his greatness].

Sefer HaSichos 5702, p. 86

---

* During the part of the *Seder* known as *Yachatz*, a whole matzah is broken into two pieces, and the larger piece is put aside for the *afikomen*.

FINDING G-D

A story is told about the Maggid of Mezritch. Once, his son came running to him in tears. The Maggid comforted him and asked him why he was crying. The child began to explain that he had been playing a game of hide-and-seek with his friends.

He and all his friends were hiding. They remained in their hiding places for a long time, thinking that they had hid well, and that the person whose turn it was was unable to find them. But soon they got tired of waiting. They came out of their hiding places and found out that they had been wrong. The one whose turn it was was not even there. He had played a trick on them! After they went into their hiding places, he went home instead of searching for them. That is why the Maggid's son was crying.

When the Maggid of Mezritch heard this story, he also began to cry. His son asked him why he was crying. The Maggid told him that G-d has the same complaint.

What did the Maggid mean? It is written, "You are a G-d Who hides." G-d says, "I hide Myself from you, but the purpose of My hiding is that you should come and search for Me. But instead of searching for Me, you go away and busy yourselves with other things."

Likkutei Sippurim by Rabbi Perlow, p. 30

FLEXIBILITY

The Rebbe Rashab was once shown a painting.*

The painting, a field of wheat, had a pleasant ambiance: the sun shone brightly and a small bird stood on top of one of the wheat stalks. Many art experts were impressed by how brilliantly and realistically the scene had been captured by the artist.

A simple farmer who viewed the painting commented that it did indeed look real, except for the bird on the stalk. Although the bird was small, the weight of its body should have bent the stalk — and in the painting, the stalk stood as straight and tall as those surrounding it.

The Rebbe drew a valuable insight from this and related its profound lesson.

One's Divine service can look beautiful and give the impression of being alive. However, if it is lacking the ability to "bend" — i.e., to be submissive to G-d's will — it ceases to be real. True goodness can only be achieved by transcending the limitations of one's personal ego.

Sefer HaSichos 5696, p. 46

---

* Three different paintings were described in the original story, but only this one addresses this theme.

The Proper

FOCUS

"When I was a little boy in Lubavitch," said the Previous Rebbe, "I would often sit and stare out the window. My teacher, the *Rashbatz*, would give me guidance on how to change my nature. He would tell me: 'Why must you be in the house looking outside [i.e., at the superficiality and foolishness of the material world]; instead go outside and look in through the window [at the inner, deeper perspective of life].'"

Sefer HaSichos 5696, p. 10

GOAL SETTING

"We had a tall tree in the yard of our home," related Rebbetzin Chana, the Rebbe's mother. "The children used to climb up and would often fall down. My six-year-old Mendel'e, [the Rebbe,] would climb up and reach the top of the tree without falling. When I asked him, 'How is it that you don't fall and all the other children fail to make it to the top?' he responded, 'As they climb, they look down and get frightened and fall. When I climb, I continually look upward. As such, I don't get frightened and I don't fall down.'"

Sefer HaToldos (Rabbi Levi Yitzchok), vol. 2, p. 345

Achieving

GOALS

The story is told of a gathering of the *Rabbonim* in Petersburg during the times of the Rebbe Rashab. The meeting was in response to the government's demand that all the Jewish religious teachers and rabbis obtain certification and degrees in secular studies. Naturally, all the *Rabbonim* opposed this decree. However, the officials threatened that if they would not comply, there would be pogroms, G-d forbid.

The Rebbe Rashab spoke harshly against the decree and urged the Jews to resist it. At the end of his speech he fainted. Due to the sharpness of his words against the government's edict and also because of his protest concerning the possible pogroms, he was arrested.

When the Rebbe was later freed from prison, one of the *Rabbonim* entered the Rebbe's office and saw him crying. He said to the Rebbe, "Lubavitcher Rebbe, why are you crying? We did all we could!" The Rebbe responded, "But we were not successful in achieving our goal!!"

Likkutei Sichos, vol. 23, p. 161

GOSSIP

We have a tradition attributed to the Baal Shem Tov: When one hears an uncomplimentary report about another Jew — even if he does not know the individual referred to — he should be very deeply pained. For one of these two is certainly in the wrong: If what is being said about the individual is true, then the person being spoken about is defective; and if it is not true, then the talebearer is the one in an unhealthy situation.

HaYom Yom, entry for 12 Kislev

GRATITUDE

Once, when the Baal Shem Tov arrived in a certain village, he followed his usual practice of expressing his strong love for the simple Jews living there — and evoking from them their genuine and deeply felt belief in, and gratitude to, G-d.

There lived in that village an elderly Jewish scholar, known as a *gaon*, who had totally removed himself from worldly activities. For fifty years he had studied Torah all day and all night in isolation. He would fast and sit in his *tallis* and *tefillin* until the late afternoon prayers of *Minchah*. Only after the evening service did he allow himself to taste some bread and water.

When the *Besht* visited the *gaon* in his little corner of the *shul*, he asked the *gaon* about his health and whether his needs were being met. This was the *Besht*'s method of evoking praise to the A-lmighty in the form of an answer such as, "Thank G-d, everything is fine with me." The *Besht* was, as yet, unknown as the great spiritual master that he would soon be revealed to be. The *gaon*, therefore, preferring to remain undisturbed with his learning — and not recognizing the greatness of the *Besht* — ignored him.

The *Besht* persisted with the same question until the *gaon* got angry and pointed to the door (for the *Besht* to leave). The *Besht* told the *gaon*, "Why don't you give Hashem His *parnassah* (sustenance)?"

Upon hearing these cryptic words from an unknown peasant, the *gaon*'s irritation increased.

The *Besht* read the thoughts of the *gaon* and explained to him: "The Jews exist on the sustenance with which G-d provides them. On what sustenance does G-d dwell?" Answering his own question, the *Besht* continued: "King David recounts in *Tehillim* (22:4): 'And You, Holy One, are enthroned upon the praises of Israel.' The praises that Jews give to G-d, my brother, are His sustenance."

Chassidic Discourses, vol. 2, p. 256
Likkutei Sichos, vol. 7, pp. 135-136

HASTINESS

A chassid related: I once sat in the Torah study hall of Rabbi Moshe Posner, the great-grandfather of the Alter Rebbe, and was studying with great concentration. By nature I studied very quickly and in a loud voice, and I understood the material clearly.

The Alter Rebbe, continued the chassid, sat in one of the nearby libraries. When I passed him, he told me that I am learning with great desire, but too quickly. I told the Alter Rebbe that it is my nature to be quick. He responded that I must change my nature. When I told him that I cannot, he responded: A Jew has the tools to change his nature and he can accomplish this through *kabbalas ol* (submitting to the yoke of Heaven). When one gets accustomed [to this new behavior,] it becomes second nature, and the nature that is created thereby changes one's innate nature. *Kabbalas ol* is the foundation of Torah and one's G-dly service.

The Alter Rebbe continued: Your desire to study Torah is a gift from Above. In the passage "*Vaavadetem meheirah mei'al haaretz hatovah, asher A-donai nosein lachem* — And you will swiftly perish from the good land that the L-rd gives you," the word *eretz* ("land") is connected to the word *ratzon* ("desire"), which alludes to the will and desire in studying Torah and serving G-d. And when G-d gives "the good land," i.e., a desire and will to study Torah, it must be "*Vaavadetem meheirah*," i.e., one must destroy and rid himself of "*meheirah*" (hastiness), and study Torah in delight to give pleasure to the *neshamah*.

Sefer HaSichos 5700, p. 59

HEALING

The Previous Rebbe writes: "My grandmother, Rebbetzin Rivkah, once developed a lung ailment. The doctor of the city of Vitebsk 'wrote her off' [as being incurable]. She then went to her father-in-law, the Tzemach Tzedek, and he interpreted the Talmudic expression 'From here we deduce that permission is given to the practitioner to heal.' The Rebbe explained, 'The practitioner is only given permission from on High to heal, but as for any other advice, he has no say.'"

Sefer HaSichos 5705, p. 8

Good

HEALTH

A noted scholar visited the Rebbe during the *shiva* period of the Rebbe's beloved wife, Rebbetzin Chaya Mushka, o.b.m. At that time the visitor urged the Rebbe to guard his health and well-being because of his importance to so many people.

The visitor uttered the request reluctantly since it could have been interpreted as an expression of *chutzpah*. Yet he mustered the courage to express his concern bolstered by the *semichah** he had received from great Torah scholars of the previous generation.

The Rebbe responded by quoting the words of his father-in-law: "The sign of a healthy person is one who does *not* feel himself. For otherwise, the mere 'feeling' of his own physical being would be indicative of a deficiency in his health and a silent call for help. Better that I should *not* have to watch my health at all, since from the outset I will be healthy."

The *Talmud* states: One who "feels" his head (because of a headache) should preoccupy himself in Torah study. If the *Talmud* recommends this remedy for someone already suffering, how much more so does this remedy apply when preventing an ache.

Toras Menachem / Menachem Tziyon, vol. 1, p. 153

* Rabbinic ordination.

A Happy

HOME

The Rebbe was once approached by a man who asked him to verify the custom of a man folding up his *tallis* soon after Shabbos as a blessing for *shalom bayis* (peace in the home).

Chassidim say that the Rebbe replied: I can't say whether this aids in enhancing peace in the home; however, I am certainly convinced that when a husband rolls up his sleeves and washes the dishes remaining from Shabbos, *that* is a definite blessing for *shalom bayis*.

A contemporary story related by a chassid

HUMILITY

A brilliant and renowned scholar, exceptionally gifted and remarkably profound in his studies, came to Liozna and threw himself into the study of *Chassidus*. With his powerful intellectual propensity, he amassed, within a short time, a great and broad knowledge in *Chassidus*.

At his first *yechidus* with the Alter Rebbe, he asked: "Rebbe, what do I lack?" The Rebbe replied: "You lack nothing, for you are G-d-fearing and a scholar. You do need, however, to rid yourself of the *chametz** — awareness of self and arrogance — and to bring in matzah, which is *bittul*, renunciation of self."

HaYom Yom, entry for 27 Tammuz

---

* *Chametz* is the term used for all leavened products forbidden for use on Passover. The ability of leaven to "puff up" bread is likened to "puffing oneself up" with arrogance. Since matzah does not contain any leavening agents, it is often used as a metaphor for humility.

HYPOCRISY

A complaint was brought to the Alter Rebbe against his chassidim: "They prolong their *davening* and are careful with their performance of the *mitzvos*, but their efforts are superficial and they do not truly uphold that level of piety!"

The Alter Rebbe replied: "Is it really so; is it really so? If it is, then they are deserving of the verdict of the *mishnah* (end of *Peah* 8: 9): 'One who does not limp and is not blind, yet makes out as if he is, will not die until he becomes one of them!!' Since they act like chassidim, and act with love and fear of G-d through meditation and prolonged *davening*, then surely they will not leave this world until it is truly so!"

Toras Menachem 5711, Yud-Beis Tammuz, p. 200

HYPOCRISY (2)

Among the chassidim of the Tzemach Tzedek was a businessman whose dealings took him to the business centers of the large cities of Russia as well as to several foreign capitals. As time went by, he became increasingly uncomfortable in these environments with his long black coat and chassidic hat. Gradually, he adopted a more secular mode of dress on his business trips. Of course, he continued to travel to his Rebbe in traditional chassidic garb.

Then, one day, he appeared in Lubavitch in his businessman's attire. "Rebbe," he announced, "I've decided to put an end to my hypocritical behavior. This is how I dress on all my travels, so why delude myself and others with my chassidic clothes?"

"Reb Yankel," said the Rebbe, "do you think that I was not aware that you dress differently in Leipzig and Paris than you do in Lubavitch? But I thought that here you showed us your true self, and there you were the hypocrite...."

The Week in Review (as related by chassidim)

IDENTITY

The great Reb Zusia of Anipoli once said: When I arrive before the Heavenly Court, they will not ask me why I was not like the Patriarchs or like Moshe *Rabbeinu*. Rather, they will ask me why I was not Zusia.

Sichos Kodesh, night of Simchas Torah, 5722

INFLUENCE

When *Chassidus* was beginning to be propagated in Russia and Lithuania, the Alter Rebbe passed through the city of Shklov (a city inhabited by the opponents of Chassidism). The Rebbe ascended the platform in the city's large *shul* and in his characteristic, sing-song delivery, called out the passage (*Tehillim* 34:9): "Taste and see that G-d is good."

At that time the Rebbe was accustomed to delivering brief Torah thoughts.

His words left his heart and entered the hearts of the listeners. Subsequently numerous young men flocked toward him who later dedicated themselves to the study of *Chassidus*. Soon after, the Alter Rebbe's chassidic following grew into a vast community.

Toras Menachem 5713, vol. 3, pp. 65-66

INSPIRATION

A chassid of the Rebbe Maharash supported himself by manufacturing wheels for wagons.

Once, the chassid prepared wagon wheels for the Rebbe's carriage as a gift. He fashioned them with a deep love in his heart and with the fear that they wouldn't be beautiful enough for the Rebbe.

When they were ready, he set out for Lubavitch with the wheels. There he presented the Rebbe with his gift and said: "Rebbe, I am giving you *Ofanim** (wheels). The Rebbe should give me *Chayos HaKodesh**, i.e., inspiration in holy matters."

Igros Kodesh of the Rebbe Rayatz, vol. 5, p. 153

---

* Referring to the verse in the Morning Prayer: "*VehaOfanim veChayos HaKodesh*," literally meaning the various levels of angels.

The Power of

INTELLECT

Shortly before his *histalkus* (passing), the Rebbe Rashab asked that he be moved into the study hall where he delivered his discourses. "I am going to heaven," he told his followers, "but I am leaving my writings with you" — the writings that would keep his spirit alive for his disciples.

When his son (the Rebbe Rayatz) heard these words, he began to weep. His father, weak with illness, turned to him and said, "Emotions? Emotions? No! Intellect. Intellect." The chassidim who were there related that in one miraculous moment, the Rebbe Rayatz changed completely.

Ashkavte d'Rebbe, Rabbi Moshe DovBer Rivkin
(NY, 5713), p. 92

INTROSPECTION

When the Alter Rebbe was imprisoned, he was interrogated by a deputy-minister who was learned in Scripture and an authority on Jewish affairs.

One of the questions the official put to him concerned the plain meaning of the verse (*Bereishis* 3:9): "And G-d called to the man (Adam) and said to him, 'Where are you?'" The official asked, "Didn't G-d know where Adam was? Why did He have to inquire, 'Where are you?'"

The Alter Rebbe explained *Rashi*'s interpretation of the verse. The official, however, said, "I am aware of *Rashi's* explanation. I would like to hear an explanation from the Rabbi!"

The Alter Rebbe replied: "When a person is, for example, so-and-so many years old (and here he mentioned the exact age of his interrogator), the A-lmighty asks him: 'Where are you? Are you aware of why you were created and put on this earth? Are you aware of what you are expected to do and how much you have already accomplished?'"

Likkutei Sichos, vol. 1, p. 73

JUDGING OTHERS

The Previous Rebbe was once questioned about his efforts to befriend all Jews, even those who are the opposite of those "who are to be promoted and not to be cast down."*

The Previous Rebbe replied: "The *Shulchan Aruch* consists of four parts: *Orach Chayim, Yoreh Deah, Even Ha'ezer* and *Choshen Mishpat.* The laws concerning issues of 'promoting' appear in *Choshen Mishpat,* the final section of the *Shulchan Aruch,* and there itself it is in the very last sections.

"The order of learning is in the sequence mentioned: first one learns all sections of *Orach Chayim, Yoreh Deah* and *Even Ha'ezer,* and then nearly all of *Choshen Mishpat,* until one reaches the final few sections. Only then does he learn whether he should 'promote' or, Heaven forbid, otherwise."

The deeper meaning of this is as follows:

To do a favor for a fellow Jew is certainly a *mitzvah.* To cause someone harm, however, arguing that this act is in accordance with the Torah, may very well be based on a misinterpretation of the actual law. It is also possible that ulterior motives are involved. Moreover, he may be reprimanding the other not so much

---

* See *Avodah Zarah* 26b, where the *Gemara* enumerates the types of sinners that "may be cast down and need not be brought up (i.e., saved or promoted)," such as heretics, informers and apostates.

because the *Shulchan Aruch* demands it but simply because he enjoys castigating.

A judge must of necessity be a compassionate person, capable of finding merit in those he is judging. Even when he has to sentence the defendant to flogging, or a more severe penalty, he cannot personally carry out the sentence — even though the ruling is sound according to *Shulchan Aruch* — because of his inability to bear the other's suffering. The sentence is thus carried out by a deputy of the court.

Likkutei Sichos, vol. 1, p. 133

JUDGMENTALNESS

Reb Hillel Paritcher desired to see the Alter Rebbe, but each time he would arrive in the city that the Alter Rebbe was currently visiting, he would miss him. So he decided to make sure to arrive first at the next place the Alter Rebbe was destined to be. To further insure that he would meet the Alter Rebbe, when he arrived at the next destination, he went directly to the home where the Alter Rebbe would be staying and hid underneath the bed.

Reb Hillel prepared a question in the tractate of *Erachin* to ask the Alter Rebbe. As soon as the Alter Rebbe entered the room — even before Reb Hillel had a chance to emerge — he heard the sing-song of the Alter Rebbe: "If a *yunger man* (young man) has a question in *Erachin*, he must first be *maarich* (evaluate himself)." Immediately, Reb Hillel fainted, and by the time he was revived, the Alter Rebbe had already left.

The explanation of the story as it pertains to us is this:

Erachin, [lit., the monetary value of people as it relates to various situations in Torah law,] is illogical. The ruling is that the process of evaluation is based on a person's years, not his qualities. All people of the same age carry the same value. At first glance one may ask: "I have spent all my life engaged in Torah and Divine service, of which G-d must be very proud. Should my years not be valued higher than those of the ordinary person? The other person's years went to waste, so how could both of our years be valued as equal?"

To this we tell him: When one has a question in *Erachin* (the "Value of People"), he must first evaluate himself, and automatically his question will be resolved.

Likkutei Sichos, vol. 2, p. 401

The Wisdom of a True

LEADER

The holy Ruzhiner would not tolerate any melancholy or even bitterness — and as a result, his chassidim became quite playful. One Tishah BeAv they spent some time tossing burrs at one another. Then they decided to run up to the roof of the *beis midrash* and lower a noose over the entrance. Whoever walked in the door could then be lassoed and promptly hoisted up to the roof. The prank succeeded until, sure enough, who should walk in but — their Rebbe, the Ruzhiner. From their vantage point it was hard to tell one hat from another, and only when the *tzaddik* was halfway up did they identify him.

When they had lowered him to the ground, he exclaimed, "Master of the Universe! If Your children do not observe Your *Yom Tov*, then take it away from them!"

Sefer HaMinhagim Chabad, English ed., pp. 98-99

LIFTING SPIRITS

The widow of Jacques Lifschitz, the renowned sculptor, came for a private audience with the Lubavitcher Rebbe shortly after her husband's sudden passing. In the course of her meeting with the Rebbe, she mentioned that when her husband died, he was nearing completion of a massive abstract sculpture of a phoenix (a mythical bird that is said to have "risen from the ashes"), a work commissioned by the Hadassah Women's Organization for the Hadassah Hospital on Mt. Scopus, in Jerusalem.

As an artist and sculptor in her own right, she said that she would have liked to complete her husband's work, but, she told the Rebbe, she had been advised by Jewish leaders that the phoenix is a non-Jewish symbol. How could she complete it and allow it to be placed in Jerusalem, no less?!

One of the Rebbe's secretaries was standing near the door to the Rebbe's office that night when the Rebbe called for him and asked that he bring him the book of Job from his bookshelf, which he did.

The Rebbe turned to chapter 29, verse 18, which reads: "I will live as long as the *chol* (phoenix)."

The Rebbe then proceeded to explain to Mrs. Lifschitz the *Midrashic* commentary on this verse which describes the *chol* as a bird that lives for a thousand years, dies, and is later resurrected from its ashes.

Clearly, the phoenix *is* a Jewish symbol.

Mrs. Lifschitz was absolutely delighted and the project was completed soon thereafter. How fitting was this beautiful metaphor of life returning from the ashes. In his own Divinely inspired way, the Rebbe had brought new hope to this broken widow, much as he has done for the spirit of the Jewish people, raising them from the ashes of the Holocaust to new, invigorated life.

To Know and To Care, vol. 2, p. 139

Creating

LIGHT

The Previous Rebbe related: As a young child I debated whether angels knew the solutions to mathematical equations. After all, they know everything; perhaps they knew this too? I then asked my father, the Rebbe Rashab. My saintly father clarified it for me and went on to say that one thing is certain: The angel Michoel makes an accurate reckoning of all the chapters of *Tehillim* people recite, and with it he fashions a beautiful chandelier which serves to illuminate the heavenly realms as well as this world for the person and for all his future generations.

Although I was still young, my father would often ask me, "What's doing with the chandelier?"

Sefer HaSichos 5709, p. 336

LIVING IN THE MOMENT

The construction of the *Mishkan* (the Holy Tabernacle) has a lesson to teach us in our daily lives. When the Jewish people were traveling in the desert, some of their stopovers lasted only one day or night. Nonetheless, at every stop they reassembled the *Mishkan* with all its details just as they did at a place where they spent eighteen years.

This is a lesson for each and every Jew in how to conduct himself in his service to G-d and the pursuit of his mission in this world. One should not consult the calendar or the clock to estimate if what he is about to do will last for eighteen years. Nor should he think that if whatever he is doing is unlikely to endure for more than a single day or night then perhaps it is not worth the effort. For just as G-d is eternal and unlimited and undefined by time, so, too, all the actions of a Jew that are connected with his service to G-d are eternal — even if in a few minutes he will find himself involved in another pursuit.

Igros Kodesh of the Rebbe, vol. 10, p. 107

LUST

Reb Shmuel Munkis, a chassid of the Alter Rebbe, was one of those present at a *farbrengen* of chassidim. He was known to all as the jokester who was always on the jolly side. It once occurred that roasted lungs (a delicacy) were brought to the *farbrengen* as an appetizer to accompany the *l'chaims*. Reb Shmuel was the one charged to distribute the exotic meat to those assembled.

He jumped around with the tray of meat on the palm of his hand and was extremely annoying to those whose tongues were anxious to taste it. His bizarre behavior made them want to put him on the table and give him a good-natured thrashing! But Reb Shmuel danced around with it until finally he dumped it into the trash.

A little while later, the butcher came running in frantically. "Do not eat the meat! The meat is not kosher!" Through a misunderstanding, his wife had mistaken this piece of non-kosher meat for kosher, and had given it to them by mistake. The butcher wanted to be sure that the chassidim did not partake of the meat.

This even intensified the feelings of those assembled toward Reb Shmuel. "How did you know that the meat was non-kosher? Are you practicing *ruach hakodesh* (Divine inspiration) in revealing things the ordinary person does not know? What gives you the right to do that?" At this point, they really wanted to get back at him for his outlandish behavior.

Reb Shmuel responded, "I have learned from my mentor, the Alter Rebbe, the following: Only something that is prohibited creates such strong pangs of desire, whereas something permissible does not get the person so excited. When the meat arrived, I had a tremendous longing for it and I also saw this lust on the faces of those assembled, so I instinctively knew from my studies with the Alter Rebbe that I must not allow myself or others to partake of this prohibited craving!"

So I was keeping my promise "not to enjoy a material pleasure!"

Sefer HaSichos 5703, p. 176

MATERIALISM

Once, as a child, the Mitteler Rebbe was asked to explain why the assembled chassidim appeared morose. He replied, "It is clearly alluded to in our prayers: '*Atzabeihem kesef vezahav...*' (their *idols* are of silver and gold, the handiwork of man). The word '*atzabeihem*' can also be interpreted as: 'Their *depression* stems from silver and gold, (i.e., because their thoughts are focused on acquiring another ruble).'"

Sefer HaSichos 5705, p. 108

There is an expression: "The word *gelt*, געלט (money) has the same numerical value (112) as the word *blote*, בלאטע (mud)." The Rabbis teach us, "Gold was created for the building and the vessels of the Holy Temple."

[In order to reconcile both sayings,] we must know how to interpret them. When one uses money for his physical desires, the money is likened to mud. However, when one uses money for a spiritual purpose, then the money is properly used.

Sefer HaSichos 5703, p. 10

What

MATTERS

A chassid (Reb Shmuel Levitin)* once related a story about his imprisonment in Siberia. He was deprived of any holy books with which to pray and study, and when it came to the morning blessing "הנותן ליעף כח — He Who gives the weary strength," he was unsure whether the word was "ליעף" or "לעיף," even though both words mean the same thing.

The Rebbe commented: The only thing this chassid had on his mind while in the worst of places was the above question, and the only thing that remained with him twenty years after he was liberated was the memory of this struggle.

We can easily see the impact of a Rebbe on his chassid in spite of suffering and constant struggle when we witness what remains the priority in the chassid's life when all is said and done: how to pronounce a word in *davening*.

Sichos Kodesh 5734, Elul 18

---

* The Rebbe said this a few days after Reb Levitin's passing on 11 Elul.

MEDITATION

The Rebbe relates: "I heard from chassidim of Poland that when the Rebbe of Modzitz fell ill and traveled to Berlin for medical advice, the doctors said he would need to have surgery. However, since he was extremely weak, they were unsure if he could survive the pain of surgery, [since in those days there was no anesthesia]. When the Rebbe heard this, he said they should wait until he would sing a melody and enter into a trance. As is known, he had great melodic power, and from his deep concentration in the delight of the melody he would not feel what was happening. Then they would be able to perform the surgery without concern. So it was. They waited until he entered into a melodic trance, they performed the surgery, and all went well.

"We see from this that even in our generation it is possible for a Jew to meditate on a pleasant experience to the extent that he does not feel what is happening to and around him."

Likkutei Sichos, vol. 27, p. 275

MOODINESS

Life does not always go smoothly. Just as a person's [mood or circumstances] can go up, there is also the possibility that they can go down. One need not be shaken and forlorn when he does experience a downturn in mood or status, especially when it only involves material matters, and particularly when he knows that he has no control over these things. This downturn should serve as impetus to strengthen and deepen his trust and belief in G-d — so much so that an outside observer would see that he is the stronger for it and does not get shaken by undesirable outcomes in his life, especially since it is only for a short period of time.

Igros Kodesh of the Rebbe, vol. 8, p. 129

The Truth About

MOTIVATION

It was on a very rainy day that the Baal Shem Tov was sitting in *yeshivah* with his students — deep in prayer and study — when a passing wagon got stuck in deep mud. The gentile wagon driver poked his head in the window of the *yeshivah* and requested help. Seeing that the wagon was sunk knee-deep in mud, they told him that they did not have the strength to successfully retrieve the wagon. The gentile responded with a Russian expression: "Able, you are able. You just don't want. And when people don't want, they pretend that they are not able."

The Baal Shem Tov explained to his students: "We must learn from the wagon driver's statement how to better serve G-d. The Torah tells us we must always work to enhance our learning — but sometimes one believes that he doesn't have the ability because he feels tired. The truth is, we must learn from this person's response that, 'Able, we are able,' for G-d grants us the strength to accomplish all good things. But because we are influenced by our negative drives, we tell ourselves that we are not able."

Sichos Kodesh 5720, 15 Tammuz

Life's True

NECESSITIES

"The needs of Your people are great, and their knowledge is scant" (*Neilah* service of Yom Kippur).

The Rebbe Maharash interprets this statement as follows: Why are their needs great? Because their knowledge is scant (i.e., narrow and limited).

We can derive two points from this:

The first is that the individual is not giving proper value to his essence — his spiritual being. As a result, he is on a constant search for more and more physical pleasures and luxuries, not realizing that this causes him to risk losing what he has and not be granted his true (spiritual) needs. The Tzemach Tzedek once compared this to oversized garments: not only don't they serve their ordinary purpose but they get ensnared in the wearer's legs and impede his walking altogether.

When a person develops a broad mind through the study of G-dly wisdom, however, materialism and the limitations of the physical world don't affect him, for material substance is of no significance to him. His desire and search are for spiritual values, and physicality matters to him only insofar as it relates to learning Torah and fulfilling its *mitzvos*.

Likkutei Sichos, vol. 1, p. 176

Missed

OPPORTUNITIES

Shortly before the onset of Shabbos, the Holy *AriZal* escorted his students to the outskirts of the city of Tzfas to greet the Shabbos Queen. While they were chanting their holy melodies, the *AriZal* asked his students: "My dear friends, would you like to spend Shabbos in Jerusalem?" Rather than jumping at the chance to accompany their saintly teacher on a holy mission, they hesitated, citing the Talmudic expression, "Let us go and consult our wives."

At this lack of enthusiasm and excitement, the *AriZal* became very shaken, clapped his hands together and said: "Woe onto us that we missed an opportunity to be redeemed from exile. If all of you would have unanimously embraced my invitation to travel immediately to Jerusalem with joy, we would have had the merit to greet *Mashiach* — and immediately all the Jewish people would have been redeemed. For now was a perfect moment for redemption. And since you have refused, we are back to where we were."

Toras Menachem 5718, vol. 2, p. 291, Parshas Shemini

The Pitfalls of

PERFECTIONISM

[As you set out to serve G-d,] do not be overly exacting in all you do. [To do so] is but a contrivance of the *yetzer [hara]* (the negative drive) to make you apprehensive and depressed at the thought of not having fulfilled your obligation [perfectly]. Depression, in turn, is an immense obstacle to one's service of the Creator.

Even if you did commit a sin [Heaven forbid], do not be overly depressed, lest this stop your worship. Do feel saddened by the sin [and feel ashamed before the Creator, and beg Him to remove the negativity you have drawn upon yourself]; but rejoice in the Creator, because you have fully repented and resolved never to repeat your folly.

Even if you are certain that you did not fulfill some obligation because of a variety of obstacles, do not feel depressed. Bear in mind that the Creator "searches the hearts and minds" (*Psalms* 7:10). He knows that you wished to do the best, but were unable to do so. Thus strengthen yourself to rejoice in the Creator.

Tzava'at HaRivash,
The Testament of Rabbi Israel Baal Shem Tov, p. 15

PERSISTENCE

The theme of Pesach Sheni* (lit., the "second Passover") is that it is never too late. It is always possible to put things right. Even if one was *tamei* (ritually impure), or one was far away, and even in a case of *lachem* — when this (impurity, etc.) was deliberate — nonetheless he can correct it.

HaYom Yom, entry for 14 Iyar

---

* In the first year of the Jews' forty-year sojourn in the desert, certain Jews were unable to properly fulfill their Passover obligations. In response to their cry, "Why should we be denied the privilege of bringing the offering?" G-d established Pesach Sheni to give them the opportunity to fulfill their obligations a month later.

Advice for

PERSONAL GROWTH

In bemoaning one's spiritual growth, one needs to know that part of an organized discipline and service of G-d is not to allow himself to become overburdened with unfounded demands. For just as one is to recognize his deficiencies, he must also be fully aware of his positive traits. Additionally, in order to grow, a person must be in a good disposition and mood and not constantly deride himself.

He who works to better himself may encounter times that he possesses certain shortcomings. Yet — because he wants to grow and does not want this weakness to hinder his spiritual advancement — if he cannot chase away this negative trait and uproot it entirely at that moment, he should circle it with many barriers and fences so that no actual negativity will result from it. The work of chasing it away and totally ridding himself of it should be left for a later time when he will have the fortitude to achieve this task. For these are precisely the two components necessary for organized and well-structured discipline: one, to recognize one's weaknesses and yet, two, to continually encourage and boost his morale to move forward and grow.

Igros Kodesh of the Rebbe Rayatz, vol. 7, p. 320

Proper

PLANNING

A story is told of a man who wanted to write a will, leaving an extremely large sum of money to Torah institutions after his passing. He asked the Rebbe Rashab how he should proceed. The Rebbe answered that instead of figuring out and worrying how his money should be spent after his long life, he would do better to give charity during his long and healthy years. That way, he would derive pleasure and enjoyment from seeing how the institution benefited from his charity immediately.

Sefer HaSichos 5697, vol. 2, p. 188;
Toras Menachem 5711, vol. 2, p. 189

Finding the

POSITIVE IN
THE NEGATIVE

The Alter Rebbe himself was the Torah reader in their *shul* in Liozna. Once, the Alter Rebbe had to be away from Liozna on the Shabbos of *Parshas Savo*, and the Mitteler Rebbe, then not yet *bar mitzvah*, heard the Torah reading from someone else. The Mitteler Rebbe's anguish at the curses in the *Tochachah* (the section of admonition) caused him so much heartache, that on the following Yom Kippur the Alter Rebbe doubted whether his son would be able to fast.

When they asked the Mitteler Rebbe, "Don't you hear this *parshah* every year?" he replied, " When Father reads, one doesn't hear any curses."

HaYom Yom, entry for 17 Elul

POSSESSION

Once, as the Alter Rebbe stepped out of his room, he overheard his wife remarking to several women, "Mine (i.e., my husband) says...."

The Alter Rebbe said: "With one *mitzvah* I am yours; with how many [*mitzvos*] are we G-d's!"

HaYom Yom, entry for 23 Shvat

PRAYER

The Tzemach Tzedek's son, Reb Yosef Yitzchak, was a son-in-law of the great Reb Yaakov Yisrael Tsherkaser. When Reb Yaakov Yisrael asked his son-in-law about his *davening* [i.e., whether he *davened* at length or *davened* with the *minyan*], he responded that he tried to pray with a *minyan*. Reb Yaakov Yisrael was pleased with the answer.

Once, Reb Yaakov Yisrael sent someone to summon Reb Yosef Yitzchak to him, but the messenger found him involved in prayer. This caused Reb Yaakov Yisroel to wonder, since the *minyan* had already finished praying. Soon after, he again summoned his son-in-law but he was still in the middle of his prayers. This continued several times and much time elapsed. When Reb Yosef Yitzchak finished praying, Reb Yaakov Yisroel asked him: "Didn't you tell me that you try to pray with a *minyan*?" Reb Yosef Yitzchak answered: "I heard from my father, in the name of the Alter Rebbe, that the concept of praying with a *tzibbur* (*minyan*) is *litzbor*, to gather together all the forces of the soul and all its G-dly sparks. This takes a long time."*

Likkutei Sichos, vol. 2, p. 477

---

* Author's Note: This story is not meant in any way to give us license to forego the *halachic* mandates of *davening* with a *minyan* (a quorum of ten men), rather it is describing a deeper dimension of praying with a *tzibbur*.

PRAYER

One of the adherents of the Alter Rebbe was such a simple chassid that people doubted his knowledge of the meaning of the prayers. Nonetheless he prayed at length, even during the weekday prayers.

The chassidim were amazed that, in spite of his simplicity, he prayed with great depth and fervency. They questioned him about this.

"I only know that which I heard from the [Alter] Rebbe: *'Zachor v'shamor bedibur echad* — [The words] "remember" and "guard" [the Shabbos] (were uttered by G-d) in one breath.' The Rebbe interpreted this to mean: One must remember and guard in one's every utterance (breath) the *echad*, the oneness of G-d," he responded.

It was with this Torah thought from the [Alter] Rebbe that he prayed for forty consecutive years.

Sefer HaSichos 5696, p. 127; Likkutei Sichos, vol. 14, p. 224

PURPOSE

Whoever has faith in individual Divine Providence knows that "Man's steps are established by G-d"; that this particular soul [came down to this world to] purify and improve something specific in a particular place. For centuries, or even since the world's creation, that which needs purification or improvement waits for this soul to come and purify or improve it. The soul too, has been waiting — ever since it came into being — for its time to descend, so that it can discharge the tasks of purification and improvement assigned to it.

HaYom Yom, entry for 3 Elul

QUALITY OF LIVING

When the Alter Rebbe wished to bless R. Yekusiel Liepler with wealth, the latter said he did not want it — he did not want wealth distracting him from studying *Chassidus* and performing his G-dly service. When the Rebbe wished to bless him with longevity, he answered, "But not with 'peasant years' — men who have eyes but do not see, who have ears but do not hear; who neither perceive nor hear G-dliness."

HaYom Yom, entry for 6 Cheshvan

RATIONALIZATION

A Jew once came to the city of Lubavitch and approached the Rebbe Rashab with a debate:

"You think it is a big deal to sit in (the city of) Lubavitch, closed up in a room, and behave as a fine Jew?! To roam the streets of Petersburg and not to sin — that is a big deal!

"And if you think *that* is a big deal, to sit in a Petersburg theater with closed eyes and not sin — *that* is a big deal!

"And if that is not enough, to sit in a Petersburg theater with *open* eyes and not sin — *that* is a big deal!

"And if that is not enough, to sit in a Petersburg theater and come close to the stage where the actors are playing and still not sin — *that* is a big deal!!"

And so he continued with a long list of things. One can only imagine down which road this type of thinking and rationalization leads!

Likkutei Sichos, vol. 18, p. 461

Rationalization (2)

As for self-pity, it is viewed as one of the most cunning lures of the negative drive within man. One may lament: "Since G-d created me this way, since my condition is such and such, since I am a more pitiable character than anyone else — it is impossible to do anything about [my faults] and I am exempt from [being accountable] to anyone or anything!"

In order that others should not voice their complaints about him (e.g., "How is it that he is such and such ...!?") he prefaces by saying, "I am a good person and I have no complaints, and I cannot do anything [about who I am]. And even if you think that I *can* do something [about my negative traits] but I don't want to — I say this [too] is my nature and there is nothing to do about this. I know all the complaints about me; however, this is my nature and therefore [that's the way it goes]."

One must know, "If you have toiled and not succeeded, you may not be believed"* (i.e., one should then question the nature of one's "toil").

Kuntres Tzaddik LaMelech, vol. 7, p. 362

---

* *Talmud, Megillah 6b.*

REACHING OUT
TO OTHERS

The Mitteler Rebbe was once in Homil visiting the known chassid Reb Aizil of Homil on the Intermediate Days of Passover. The Mitteler Rebbe's chassidim in that town bemoaned to him that Reb Aizil was not befriending them and was only involved in his own life.

The Mitteler Rebbe asked him: "Why are you not reaching out to the youngsters in your community and teaching them *Chassidus*?"

Reb Aizil responded: "If I don't have a quiet moment to work on myself, then how can I work with someone else?"

The Mitteler Rebbe replied: "Aizil, Aizil do as I do! When I see that I cannot have an effect on myself, should I then be a total waste? At least let me do a favor for someone else."

Shmuos v'Sippurim, vol. 2, p. 155

SECURITY

One should deeply meditate on the fact that G-d guides and gives life to the whole world, and to each and every one of us individually. This should remove worry from our hearts, for surely G-d causes the best to happen, and this does not depend on us. The one thing that *does* relate to us is our free choice to study Torah and perform *mitzvos*.

This is not my invention, for this matter is simple and known to all. However, if this attitude is external to us, and when it comes to our actual conduct we act as if everything is contingent upon and controlled by us, this causes useless heaviness in our hearts and our lives. In contrast, when we are permeated with the belief that "G-d is my Shepherd," then even the body and the animal soul feel the "I shall not lack."*

Igros Kodesh of the Rebbe, vol. 4, p. 189

---

* *Psalm* 23.

Security (2)

Rabbi Meir of Premishlan's trek to immerse in the *mikveh* attracted much attention. The *mikveh* was situated at a point in a river on the slope of a tall mountain. When the road was icy, the people had to detour around the mountain so as not to slip. Rabbi Meir, however, would march straight up the mountain and would never falter. When asked by some youngsters the secret to his success he responded:

"When one is connected Above, one does not fall down!"

Toras Menachem 5711, vol. 2, p. 105

Self-Assessment

A businessman must periodically take inventory, balance his accounts, and determine his financial standing. Regular accounting procedures keep a business running smoothly and are a pillar of successful commerce.

However, most of his time is spent engaged in commercial activity. He pauses only to evaluate a particular transaction, to ascertain if it will be profitable, and to determine the best approach. The examination of the overall status of his business is conducted far less frequently, usually only once a year, for were it to be done every day, there would be no time to conduct any actual transactions.

We should follow the same procedures in our service to G-d, which is our "business." Most of the time — our "business year" — we deal in the "commodities" of Torah and *mitzvos*. Only the month of Elul, which precedes Rosh HaShanah and Yom Kippur, is the time for a "general financial review" — when we concentrate on introspection, stocktaking and spiritual accounting.

For the rest of the year, we should pause only briefly for specific, short-range assessments. For example, upon reciting the *Shema* each evening before retiring, we sum up the credits and debits, the achievements and deficiencies of that day; before Shabbos, we examine the accounts of the previous week; and before *Rosh Chodesh* (the beginning of a new month), we balance the account for the preceding month. Then, in the last month of the year, we make a comprehensive analysis of the entire year.

Some people believe that to proceed with Torah and *mitzvos*, they must know exactly where they stand at every moment and constantly reexamine whether they are proper candidates for spiritual service, with the accompanying detailed introspection. In reality, this approach is merely a ploy of the *yetzer hara* to deflect a person from appropriate action by involving him in obsessive self-analysis. He can instead proceed on his course with confidence, leaving aside this activity until its proper time.

One may ask: "Why shouldn't a person make a general accounting each day? After all, isn't a reckoning a positive thing?" He even brings proof from *Tanya* (ch. 29; *Iggeres HaTeshuvah*, ch. 11): "My shortcomings must *always* be before me." We then inform this person: this is a ploy of the *yetzer hara*. If he would constantly be taking stock of his behavior, the majority of his time would be spent on this purpose and he would lose all his time [and become depressed — which would defeat the purpose]. Subsequently, he would not [have time to] study Torah and perform *mitzvos*, etc.

As was related by the Rebbe Rashab: "Once, someone was found crying on Simchas Torah. He did not cry when reciting *Al Cheit* on Yom Kippur, so he was making up for it two weeks later. However, that was not the proper time." "G-d made man straight." For everything there is a designated time, and for stocktaking, the proper time is the month of Elul.

Likkutei Sichos, vol. 2, p. 629; vol. 9, p. 303

SELF-CONCERN

A chassid once came to the Alter Rebbe bemoaning his financial condition and physical health: "I need G-d to grant a recovery for me as well as for my wife and family; I need to have a livelihood to pay up my debts, marry off my children, and make home improvements."

"You say all that you need. That which you are needed *for* you don't inquire!" replied the Rebbe.

Sefer HaSichos 5703, p. 195

SELF-CONTROL

A chassid of the Maggid of Mezritch once requested guidance from his teacher as to how to attain self-control. The Maggid sent him to the great Reb Zev Volf of Zhitomir. As soon as he arrived at Reb Zev's home, he knocked at the door but there was no response. Only after a prolonged period of time did someone answer the door.

As he entered the home of this great *tzaddik*, he found him holding a broom in his hand. He watched as Reb Zev busied himself with cleaning the house and performing other household tasks. Only afterwards did he receive the chassid. Reb Zev did not ask why the chassid paid him a visit nor did the chassid mention anything of this nature. The chassid felt that if the Rebbe sent him there, he would certainly be taught a lesson in how to reach a state of self-control.

Several days passed and the chassid saw nothing that struck him as instructional in this regard. Finally the chassid said to Reb Zev, "I had an audience with my Rebbe, the Maggid, and requested guidance regarding self-control. The Maggid sent me to you, but I have yet to discern any behavior on your part that would give me direction in this area!"

The *tzaddik* Reb Zev replied: "What? You haven't seen anything yet? The very moment you arrived here I showed you how one can be in control of himself: the first thing is to open the door only for whomever he chooses. The second lesson is that from time to time, one must clean out the dirt that has accumulated inside. Do these lessons not suffice for you?!!"

Oros B'Afeila, p. 130

Purposeful

SELF-DENIAL

In 1798, when the Czarist authorities came to take the Alter Rebbe to prison, the Alter Rebbe went into hiding. Later, when the authorities came for him a second time, the Alter Rebbe asked one of his chassidim, Reb Shmuel Munkis, what to do: Should he continue hiding or give himself up? Reb Shmuel told him to turn himself in.

"But," the Alter Rebbe countered, "isn't there a chance that I will be risking my life by being jailed?"

Reb Shmuel replied, "Rebbe, if you are truly a Rebbe, they won't be able to hurt you. And if you are not truly a Rebbe, how could you have deprived so many of your followers the physical pleasures of this world?!"*

Toras Menachem 5711, vol. 1, p. 93; ibid. 5710, p. 171

---

* In speaking about the Previous Rebbe on *Yud-Beis* Tammuz (the birthday and day of liberation of the Previous Rebbe from prison), the Rebbe told the above story (in 5711 — 1951) and then explained: For thousands of Jews, the [Previous] Rebbe removed (or at least diminished) their relish in the pleasure of worldly delights. Why? In order to enable them to arrive at a knowledge of G-dliness; to "know the G-d of your father and serve Him with a whole heart." Accordingly, if people conduct themselves in a way that does not fulfill the Rebbe's purpose, they are left with the deprivation of relish but without any result. (*Toras Menachem 5711*)

SELF-ESTEEM

"Just as one must recognize shortcomings, so, too, one must recognize *his own* (good) qualities" (*Sefer HaSichos 5710*, p. 386).

To understand this statement — related many a time by our chassidic masters — it is important to note that the emphasis of *"his own"* is used only when addressing the (good) qualities. When mentioning the shortcomings, however, only the word "shortcomings" is stated.

The reason is that, in essence, sins and shortcomings are foreign to and don't belong to a Jew. The only reason a Jew comes in contact with sin is that he has been charged with a mission to elevate this world; thus inevitably he comes in contact with and is influenced by the negative inclination within him. However, even after he succumbs to sin, it is truly not his, but merely an extraneous matter that lingers on due to outside influences and environment.

A Jew must be aware of his quintessential essence — his goodness and kindness — for this is his true self.

Toras Menachem 5742, vol. 1, p. 53

SELF-SACRIFICE

When the Alter Rebbe was eight years old, he wrote a commentary on the Torah. This commentary was a conglomeration of the three commentaries of *Rashi*, *Ibn Ezra*, and the *Ramban*. At the age of ten he had an unusual dream, which began with him sitting in the second room of the *shul* in Liozna and studying. Suddenly Reb Reuven Baal Shem appeared to him and demanded that he appear for judgment in the *shul*. When he entered, he saw a group of judges sitting at a table and three prestigious elders standing afar. Then the middle judge motioned for all [the elders] to approach, [after which Reb Reuven Baal Shem escorted the Alter Rebbe to the table].

The judges sat wrapped in their *talleisim* and the elders were dressed in white clothing. When the elders approached, the judge situated in the middle turned to the Alter Rebbe and said: "These three elders, *Rashi*, *Ibn Ezra*, and the *Ramban*, are calling you to trial. They claim you are depriving them of the merit of sharing their teachings with others through your commentary that includes all three."

The Alter Rebbe had no words with which to reply, so he said sincerely, and with a cry, that he would burn his writings. The elders put their hands on his head and blessed him to succeed in his studies and to continue to develop innovations [in Torah] and to pave a way of service to G-d that thousands of Jews in all generations would follow until the coming of *Mashiach*.

When he awoke, he was saddened and distressed, and took upon himself a personal fast. But when he dreamed the same dream a second time, he burned his writings.

Sefer HaToldos of the Alter Rebbe, p. 8

SLANDER

The Baal Shem Tov used to instruct his disciples in a regular *Gemara* study session. He conducted the studies with great acuity and brilliance, and included a study of *Rambam, Alfasi, Rosh* and other commentaries of the *Rishonim* (early commentators) germane to the *Gemara*-text under examination. The Baal Shem Tov would translate the words (of the text) into Yiddish. When studying the passage "the third tongue (i.e., the person relating a previously heard bit of slander) kills three persons" (*Erachin* 15b), the Baal Shem Tov translated and explained: "*Lashon hara* (lit., the evil tongue — slander) kills all three, the inventor of the slander, the one who relates it, and the listener. All this takes place on the spiritual plane, but it is more severe than physical murder."

HaYom Yom, entry for 13 Cheshvan

The Power of

SPEECH

A resident of Mezhibuzh had a quarrel with another. Once, while in the Baal Shem Tov's *shul*, he shouted that he would tear the other fellow to pieces like a fish.

The Baal Shem Tov told his pupils to hold one another's hands, and to stand near him with their eyes closed. Then he placed his holy hands on the shoulders of the two disciples next to him. Suddenly the disciples began shouting in great terror: They had seen that fellow actually dismembering his disputant.

This incident shows clearly that every [thought and spoken word] has an effect — either in physical form or on a spiritual plane — that can be perceived only with higher and more refined senses.

HaYom Yom, entry for 29 Tishrei

SUCCESS

Those who reach out to inspire our fellow Jews and bring them closer to Judaism may sometimes feel that they have not succeeded the way they would have liked. They need but think of the *mitzvah* of burning *chametz* on *erev* Passover. The actual *mitzvah* consists of *searching* for the *chametz*, and even if one has not found anything, his blessing was still not in vain.

Among the many accomplishments of reaching out to our fellow Jews — although one may feel that he has not succeeded in his journeys — is the following: Imagine a Jew is sitting in his home looking out the window and sees a young man with a beard running by. He is reminded of his father and how his father taught him to wake up saying the words of the *Modeh Ani* and recite the *Shema* prayer prior to retiring at night. And at that very moment he recalls verbally, or at least in thought, the words of these prayers.

The mere fact that a young man with a beard is running around to arouse the hearts of his fellow Jews — this alone surely has a positive effect on the surrounding environment.

Likkutei Sichos, vol. 2, p. 369

SUFFERING

In response to a letter, the Rebbe writes: Regarding your remarks about the suffering and losses in your life, I wish to draw an analogy that perhaps will shed some light on the issue at hand.

It is an experience indeed to enter an operating room in a hospital and witness a human being crying out in pain, lying on the operating table, surrounded by people with knives in their hands who are cutting him.* Not knowing the patient's medical history, the onlookers would be frantic, thinking that murderers are attacking a victim who is weeping from great pain.

However, when these same observers are informed of the prolongation of life the surgery is expected to bring, they will then focus their attention on how the process is healing the patient rather than viewing the surgeons as cold murderers.

The same is true regarding the turbulent moments in one's life, when undesirable and even unfortunate things happen. If one believes that the world is not a jungle in which things just randomly happen, but that things are run by a system that governs not only his life but his family's too, he will become confident that his experiences are part of the overall Divine system that controls every element of Creation. The only unfulfilled desire that he may still have is that he does not hear a message directly from the

---

* This refers to minor surgeries which were then performed without anesthesia.

Instructor, namely G-d, as to the rhyme and reason for all that transpires in his life.

Igros Kodesh of the Rebbe, vol. 13, p. 171

The Power of

THOUGHT

At the evening meal on Shemini Atzeres in Riga, the Previous Rebbe addressed his chassidim in the *sukkah*: "Thoughts are powerful. Not only is thought the first and innermost of the three garments (*levushim*) of the soul to which thought is united, thinking actually produces results that can extend into the realm of action. Concentrating on a good thought concerning another is in itself an act — though it is an act only in the context of the world of thought. It still needs to pass through the succeeding stages of speech and practical action."

At this point the subject turned to the members of the chassidic brotherhood who were then in Russia, and some of the past and present *yeshivah* students (*temimim*) and older chassidim (*Anash*) were mentioned by name.

The Rebbe proceeded: "Thought knows no bounds. No partition can stand in its way, and at all times it reaches its required destination."

One of those present, who had recently reached Riga from Russia, then asked: "But what benefit does the other party have from that?"

"He benefits in rich measure," replied the Rebbe.

After a long pause the Rebbe turned to the questioner and asked: "And where were *you* last Sukkos...?"*

Likkutei Dibburim, vol. 1, p. 2

---

* It was the custom of the Rebbe of each generation to bring to mind each of his chassidim at certain times. The only reason this chassid was able to get out of Russia is that the Rebbe had him in his thoughts.

CHASSIDIC SOUL REMEDIES **133**

The Proper Use of

TIME

The *Talmud* relates the words of Rabbi Yochanan ben Zakkai uttered in the moment just prior to his passing: "I don't know in which direction I will be led," (i.e., whether he would go to Heaven or the opposite).

How can we understand this uncertainty from a spiritual giant such as Rabbi Yochanan? Because of his preoccupation with fulfilling his mission in this world — in which he was engaged up until his last second — Rabbi Yochanan had no time to examine or evaluate — let alone pride himself in — his spiritual accomplishments.

He knew that if he would squander even one moment that could have been devoted to performing *mitzvos* or strengthening his knowledge of Torah, he could be considered rebellious against G-d by not fulfilling his mission to the best of his ability.

Toras Menachem 5712, vol. 1, p. 332

TOIL

A chassid once spoke privately with the Rebbe the Tzemach Tzedek, bemoaning the fact that he had no desire to learn. The Rebbe said in response, "So what should I do, given that I *do* have a desire to learn?"*

One must learn Torah through toil. Thus when one begs for a desire to learn, he is giving away a great opportunity: the merit of *not* having a desire. So when he learns out of *kabbalas ol* (submission to the yoke of Heaven) and through toil, he will reach great delight. Instead he gives away his delight and all that it entails and asks for a desire!

Likkutei Sichos, vol. 15, p. 503

---

* Having been born with an innate desire to learn, the Tzemach Tzedek was not able to earn the higher level of merit achieved by learning for its own sake (as opposed to learning out of desire).

TOIL (2)

Once, when the Rebbe Maharash was traveling through Berditchev, he saw a group of elderly Tolna chassidim carrying buckets of water and scrubbing the walls and floor of a little *shul* in preparation for a visit from their Rebbe the following day.

When the Rebbe asked them why they were doing all the work themselves instead of letting the younger chassidim help them, they answered, "We are doing this ourselves because we want to have healthy angels to assist the advocating angels who come out of the *tekios*, the blasts of the *shofar*."

One of them explained: "You know the *Yehi Ratzon* that is said after the *tekios* of Rosh HaShanah — the one that mentions 'the angels that are formed from the blowing of the *shofar*, and from the *tekia*, the *shevarim*, the *teruah*, and the *tekiah*, (*kshr"k*),' [the identifying letters of the Hebrew words that signify the various sounds of the *shofar*]? Well, one Rosh HaShanah the holy Rav of Berditchev said: 'Sweet Father, compassionate Father! Just in case the angels that proceed from the *shofar* that Levi Yitzchak the son of Sarah has just blown are weak angels, let their place be taken by the holy, healthy angels that were created by the toil of Your people in preparation for Passover, as they cleaned their kitchen utensils in order to fulfill their *mitzvah* as perfectly as possible: *kratzen* (scouring), *shobben* (scraping), *rieben* (rubbing), and *kasheren* (making kosher)!'" — [for the initials of these four Yiddish words are likewise *kshr"k*].

Likkutei Dibburim, vol. 1, p. 280

Understanding

TRAGEDY

An artist, after suffering a personal tragedy, wrote to the Rebbe about his depression and despair. The Rebbe responded: "The genius of the artist is his ability to detach himself from the external qualities of the object he is portraying, to look deeply into the object and see its essence. He must then be able to express that essence so that whoever views the painting sees an essence that he, the viewer, had never noticed in the object itself.

"The same applies to each individual: his inner essence is G-dliness. One must take great care that the secondary 'external' matters of his life should not obscure his essence and the ultimate goal and purpose of his creation. The trials, tragedies and difficulties of life must be seen for what they really are: part of the Divine system of toil and endeavor, which enables us to achieve the highest levels of happiness and goodness."

Likkutei Sichos, vol. 14, p. 253; and
a letter from the Rebbe

Making the Best of

TRAGEDY

When the Maggid of Mezritch was five years old, fire struck his parents' home and consumed it. His mother was distraught. The Maggid said to his mother, "Why are you so sad that the house was destroyed by fire, when all of us are well, thank G-d, and the house can be rebuilt?"

His mother responded, "I'm not, Heaven forbid, distressed about the house. I am saddened rather by the loss of the book of our lineage that was consumed in the fire, which traces itself back to Rabbi Yochanan HaSandler, the renowned Talmudic Sage."

"If so," answered the child, "the lineage will begin anew, with me."

Otzar Sippurei Chabad, vol. 14, p. 236

TRUTH
and Honesty

Regarding the letter that begins with the word *"Katonti,"* (printed in the *Tanya, Iggeres HaKodesh, Epistle 2*), it was said in the name of the Rebbe Maharash, passed on to the Rebbe Rashab, who in turn relayed it to the Previous Rebbe, that if the Alter Rebbe (the author) would not have inserted the three words *"b'middas emes l'Yaakov,"** ("according to the attribute of truth unto Yaakov") he would have had an additional fifty thousand chassidim, but the Rebbe demands the *middah* (trait) of *emes* (truth).

Likkutei Dibburim, vol. 1, p. 104;
HaYom Yom, 10 Menachem Av

When he would give a letter to a traveler to transport to another city, the Tzemach Tzedek would simultaneously deliver to the post office the current amount of the stamp necessary to send the letter.

Igros Kodesh of the Rebbe, vol. 11, p. 137

---

* The Alter Rebbe was demanding of his chassidim a very high level of conduct in matters of *ahavas Yisrael* (loving one's fellow Jew).

The expression of our Rebbeim is well known: In the face of *emes* (truth), all become *batel* (nullified).

Igros Kodesh of the Rebbe, vol. 17, p. 179

The Previous Rebbe writes that his father, the Rebbe Rashab, said: Truth is the middle path. An inclination to the right — to be overly stringent with oneself and find faults or sins not in accord with the truth; or an inclination to the left — to be overly indulgent, covering one's faults of leniency in demands of *avodah* (service) out of self-love — both these ways are false.

HaYom Yom, 27 Adar I

WHO ARE WE?

The Alter Rebbe held his young grandson, the Tzemach Tzedek, in his lap. The child said to his grandfather: "Zeide, Zeide!"

The Alter Rebbe asked him: "Where is Zeide?" The grandson pointed to the head of his grandfather. The Alter Rebbe said, "This is the head, not Zeide." The child then pointed to the Alter Rebbe's heart and said, "This is Zeide." The Alter Rebbe responded, "This is the heart, but not Zeide." The grandson continued to point to the other parts of the Alter Rebbe's body in order to find the place where "Zeide" is. To all these attempts, the Alter Rebbe responded that he had indicated a specific limb of Zeide, but not Zeide.

The child climbed down from his grandfather's lap and began walking around on his own. When he approached the door, he pretended that his fingers had gotten caught in the door and began to yell, "Zeide, Zeide!"

The Alter Rebbe turned to the child and said: "What is it my son; what happened?"

The child replied: "This is Zeide!!"

Otzar Sippurei Chabad, vol. 17, p. 291

WORRY

In response to a letter, the Rebbe writes: Concerning the blessing you received from my father-in-law, you have the choice whether to worry if the blessing will or won't materialize — and when it finally does materialize you will be doubly burdened as to why you wasted so much energy worrying in vain — or you may choose to be strong in your faith and trust that G-d will lead you on the straight path and fulfill all your needs. Then you will be able to say: look how well I handled the situation, that I didn't worry about things there was no reason to worry about.

Igros Kodesh of the Rebbe, vol. 4, p. 256

Maintaining

YOUTH

There is a chassidic saying on the passage: "But those who put their hope in the L-rd shall renew their vigor" (*Isaiah* 40:31). The word used to convey "renew" (*yachalifu*) [i.e., their vigor,] can also mean "to exchange" (*l'hit'chaleif*). The Jewish people make an *exchange* with G-d; they give G-d their thoughts, speech and action, and in turn G-d gives them His strengths. And because G-d's strengths are not limited or mitigated by the aging process — since aging does not apply to Him — the Jews, too, can forever be a youthful people.

Toras Menachem 5716, vol. 1, p. 108

Dedicated in partnership by

Yisroel Hakohen שיחי' **Croman**
and
Shlomo Hakohen (Steve) & Chaya (Harriet)

and their sons
Mordechai Moshe (Jake)
Adam Yehoshua (Adam)
Croman

May Heaven's blessings guide Yisroel Hakohen
together with his sons
Shlomo Hakohen and Dovid Hakohen
and their families
in all their endeavors